SOUTH WEST TRAINS

SOUTH WEST TRAINS

John Balmforth

South West Trains
John Balmforth

First published 2011

ISBN 978 0 7110 3407 5

Published by Ian Allan Publishing

an imprint of Ian Allan Publishing Ltd, Hersham, Surrey KT12 4RG.

Printed in England by Ian Allan Printing Ltd, Hersham, Surrey KT12 4RG.

Visit the Ian Allan Publishing website at www.ianallanpublishing.com

Distributed in the United States of America and Canada by BookMasters Distribution Services.

The Railway Children Charity
Registered charity No 1058991

The Railway Children Charity helps runaway and abandoned children who live in and around the world's railway stations. Working through partner organisations, the charity offers shelter, healthcare, education, training, protection and, above all, friendship.

The work of The Railway Children would not be possible without the generosity of its supporters. There are many ways you can help the charity to help the millions of street children around the world. Thanks to loyal supporters, The Railway Children now helps around 7,000 children every year, and helps, counsels or refers on about another 12,000.

All of the royalties due to the author from the sale of this book are being donated to The Railway Children charity.

You can read more about the charity on its website at www.railwaychildren.org.uk, and should you wish to support the charity, donations can be sent to:

The Railway Children
1 The Commons
Sandbach
Cheshire
CW11 1EG
United Kingdom

FRONT COVER: The future South West Trains sets Nos 444005 and 444031 await commissioning at Bournemouth TCD. *Paul S. Edwards*

BACK COVER: Unit Nos 3417, 444001 and 450001 lined up at Bournemouth TCD on the final day of Desiro acceptance trials. *Paul S. Edwards*

TITLE PAGE: Class 159/1 set No 159102 pauses at Salisbury on 5 December 2006 after arrival on the rear of the 11:20 from Waterloo, the first revenue-earning duty of the set. Having detached from the Yeovil Junction portion, the train shunted to the bay platform for public viewing of the new interior. *Brian Morrison*

OPPOSITE: SWT Class 73 electro-diesel locomotive No 73235 is captured propelling the driving car of 'Desiro' set No 444034 prior to it being loaded onto road transport for transfer to Crewe to undergo repair. *Paul S. Edwards*

Contents

Foreword

by Brian Souter
Chief Executive, Stagecoach Group

Stagecoach has often been first over the trenches when it has come to new public transport initiatives. We were one of the first to identify the potential of bus deregulation in the mid-1980s and the same was true a decade later with the privatisation of Britain's rail network.

Looking back following a period of unprecedented growth in rail travel, it is easy to forget that in the early days of privatisation there was very little interest in rail franchises. The railways were unpopular with the banks and seen as carrying significant risk. We always took a different view and could see huge opportunities in running parts of the rail network. There were many excellent British Rail managers with first-class technical knowledge. Coupled with Stagecoach's entrepreneurial ideas, we felt we had a winning formula and decided it was worth having a go.

Stagecoach won the biggest franchise, South West Trains, and ran Britain's first privatised train on 4 February 1996. We paid £1 for the right to run the franchise, probably one of the best bits of business we have ever done. It was as much down to luck as a sophisticated bid strategy. We now have more than a dozen years' experience in UK rail, but back then there was a lot we didn't understand about the railway. Still, it was the start of a new chapter in the Stagecoach story and one that has brought the company great success.

We have had a few bumps along the way, but we have learned from our early mistakes. Now we have grown to become one of the UK's most respected operators with an involvement in running around a quarter of the passenger rail market. Performance is better than it has ever been, with rising levels of customer satisfaction. We completed a major renewal of the rolling stock on the network, phasing out old slam-door Mark 1 trains and introducing a new fleet of state-of-the-art 'Desiro' trains. Not only that, the South West Trains franchise doesn't cost the government a penny. Instead, we are making a significant financial contribution to the taxpayer.

Looking to the future, I believe we need longer, more flexible rail franchises that encourage more innovation and allow operators to try new ideas. I also still believe in bringing train and track together, just as we have done at Island Line on the Isle of Wight, to deliver a more integrated railway that benefits customers.

I hope you enjoy reading the fascinating story so far at South West Trains. Our people have made it the success it is and we would not have achieved so much without them. The company is a real part of the community in London and the South West and I am delighted that the author's royalties from the book will go to the Railway Children charity, which Stagecoach has supported for a number of years.

Sitting here in 2010, we are facing fresh challenges with the tough economy and it is a difficult time for many of our own employees. But South West Trains has proved resilient in the past and I am confident it will be a blip in a longer-term trend of attracting more people out of their cars and on to greener, smarter rail travel.

Preface

by Stewart Palmer
Managing Director, South West Trains
2006-2009

Having recently retired from the role of Managing Director of the country's largest Train Operating Company after spending some 37 years on the railway I was delighted to be asked to pen a few words as the Preface to this book. South West Trains and its railway predecessors hold a very special place in my affections. I spent my latter school years in the 1960s travelling by train from New Milton to Brockenhurst to attend the grammar school. Steam-hauled of course, and we always knew when the end of the first period after lunch was coming as the 'Bournemouth Belle' went past just before the bell. In 1972 I joined British Railways as a management trainee on the South Western Division of the Southern Region, working all over the area that is now South West Trains, and after two junior management roles as Station Manager Claygate and Assistant Station Manager Surbiton, I moved away to other parts of the railway, only to eventually come back to what was by then South West Trains as Operations Director in 2000. It was like coming back to my spiritual home.

What makes this part of the network so special? I think it is several things. First of all Waterloo is a 'proper' London terminus. It has space and a real sense of arriving somewhere iconic. By 'Southern' standards the trains go long distances: Exeter, Weymouth and Portsmouth for the Isle of Wight. The main line is superbly laid out with flying junctions, and the sheer number of trains and volumes of people can make you feel proud to stand on the concourse in the rush hour when things are going well. The importance of South West Trains to the economic and social life of London cannot be overstated, with some 100,000 people relying on the company to get them to and from work in the capital every weekday. But it's not just about London; South West Trains also boasts some wonderful other destinations. Join the crowds at Ascot for the racing, on the train to Weymouth for the beach, or to Salisbury to visit the magnificent cathedral, to name just a few, and you soon realise that this railway plays an important part in the lives of the whole community – it's not just about commuting.

The whole railway industry faces considerable challenges, largely as a result of the macro-economic situation. There will be people who will, for their own purposes, say that 'things were better in the good old days'. I am firmly of the view that the railway of today is a much better railway than it was 10, 20 or 30 years ago. Of course there are things that could be better, but if you look at the reliability of the service, the frequency of services, the age and condition of the rolling stock, and the state of our stations, anybody who looks at things objectively cannot but recognise the very solid achievements of the last few years. We live, I regret to say, in the age of 'spin', but the facts speak for themselves and I am proud of what has been achieved on South West Trains. How has this happened? The one thing I can tell you is that it is not luck! It has been through hard work and attention to detail and getting the various parts of this disaggregated industry to work as one team. I want to use this opportunity to pay tribute to the fantastic people who work for South West Trains and their colleagues in Network Rail and Siemens who, by working together, have turned a railway that was not delivering to its customers into one that we can all be proud of.

Nobody can predict the future, but the railway has emerged in the last few years as part of the solution to problems of personal mobility, road congestion and climate change, not part of the problem. The environmental challenges for the country and the whole planet will play to the railway's strengths on this crowded island, and I am sure that South West Trains will play a leading role in shaping the future of travel in the areas it serves because it is a well-run business that is delivering to its customers.

CHAPTER ONE

From little acorns big oak trees grow: the birth of Stagecoach

Brother and sister team Ann and Brian Souter spent their early years growing up on a council estate at Letham, a suburb in the Scottish city of Perth. The children of a local bus driver, Iain Souter, they were destined to become famous as the founders of what eventually grew into one of the UK's largest bus and rail operators.

In 1976 Ann, in partnership with her husband Robin Gloag, set up a small company called 'Gloagtrotter', which specialised in the renting out of self-drive minibuses and motor caravans. The couple recognised the potential that expanding into the world of public transport would bring, and by 1980 had purchased a second-hand Ford Transit minibus specifically for that purpose. Brian joined his sister and her husband in March of that year after qualifying as an accountant, and it wasn't long before the company purchased its first full-size bus for use on a local Perth miners' contract. Any further expansion required a substantial investment of capital. By now the siblings' father had been made redundant from his job with Alexander (Midland), and had received a substantial redundancy package. Souter senior offered to invest £25,000 in his children's company, which by then had changed its name to GT Coaches, thus better reflecting the nature of its business. The expanded company, which would eventually change its name again, this time to Stagecoach, soon began operating long-distance motor coach services between Perth and London after the fledgling company had purchased two more second-hand motor coaches.

LEFT: Photographed at Hersham station are an SWT Class 442 'Wessex Electric' set heading south and Class 455 set No 5917 en route to Waterloo via Hounslow. *South West Trains Picture Library*

ABOVE: The first train with a Stagecoach orange stripe added to the Network SouthEast red, white and blue livery, Class 442 '5-WES' set No 2402 is displayed at Waterloo on 5 February 1996. *Brian Morrison*

It is often said that 'from little acorns big oak trees grow', and Stagecoach is an excellent example of this, ultimately expanding into what is one of the country's largest bus and rail operators. Stagecoach had also expanded internationally and by 2007 had a turnover of £1,504.6 million, giving an operating profit of £161.3 million. The Stagecoach empire still continued to grow and a brief flirtation with rail transport occurred in 1992 when the company negotiated a deal with British Rail (BR) for two fully seated Standard Class carriages painted in the Stagecoach company livery to be attached to Anglo-Scottish sleeper trains. The venture was not a success, but even so, when the government announced its intention to privatise Britain's rail network, Stagecoach was quick to identify the potential that expansion into rail offered, successfully winning the rights to operate the South West Trains (SWT) rail franchise from 4 February 1996 for a seven-year period. This was subsequently extended for a further year, being replaced by a short-term interim franchise that ran for three years to February 2007. When the franchise was re-let, the Stagecoach bid was again successful, this time seeing the company win the right to operate the services for a further 10 years up to February 2017, the last three years being subject to pre-set performance criteria being met. There was, though, a major change to the franchise's boundary as it was redrawn to combine the previous South West Trains and Island Line franchises, both of which had been operated by Stagecoach despite being separate companies in their own right. A new company, Stagecoach South Western Trains Limited, had been created as the bidding vehicle but, nevertheless, the new parent company decided to continue operating services under the South West Trains banner on the mainland and Island Line for those on the Isle of Wight.

In addition to its extensive bus network, Stagecoach Group now operates around one-quarter of the UK's passenger rail network through ownership of South West Trains; East Midlands Trains, which operates, among others, services between London and Sheffield along the Midland Main Line; and its 49% holding in the Virgin Rail Group, which operates services as West Coast Trains Ltd between London, the West Midlands and Scotland along the West Coast Main Line. Despite all this, the Stagecoach Group still retains its headquarters in its birthplace at Perth.

CHAPTER TWO

The privatisation of Britain's railways

A brief introduction

When the Conservative party under John Major's leadership won the General Election in 1992, it did so with a mandate for Britain's railways to pass into private ownership, although it did not specify in what form that should be. Many, including, it is thought, the British Railways Board, favoured using the model that had previously been used in privatising most government utilities, which would have required the railways to be sold as a single going concern, or even a return to four franchises divided in similar fashion to the pre-nationalised railway: Great Western, London Midland & Scottish, London & North Eastern, and Southern. However, in the end privatisation saw the rail infrastructure separated from the actual operation of both passenger and freight services, with a new company, Railtrack, formed to take over ownership and maintenance of the infrastructure, and many other companies, both passenger and freight, to operate the trains.

The rail network was in fact divided into 25 new franchises created to provide rail passenger services, the winners of the franchises becoming known as Train Operating Companies (TOCs). To oversee the franchising programme the Office of Passenger Rail Franchising (OPRAF) was set up and given special responsibility for letting the new franchises. For the changes to be politically acceptable, it also had to agree a core investment programme with Railtrack.

The winners of the 25 passenger franchises had to enter into track access agreements with Railtrack (these being particularly complicated where more than one company used the same

LEFT: Ageing Class 412 sets were inherited by SWT following privatisation. In this photograph Class 412 '4-BEP' set No 2317 makes a station stop at Staines on 10 October 2003. *Rich Mackin/ railwayscene.co.uk*

LEFT: Wearing the early SWT livery, Class 421 '4-CIG' set No 1882 passes through Staines on 10 October 2003. *Rich Mackin/ railwayscene.co.uk*

section of track), which in turn would allow them to use the infrastructure. The new access charges would virtually double the operating costs pertaining in British Rail days, though the theory was that the additional income would go towards bringing the infrastructure back into good order as most routes, with the notable exception of the East Coast, had not seen real investment for many years.

The TOCs would also be required to pay leasing charges to the Rolling Stock Companies (ROSCOs) for the use of the trains, ownership of which had also passed into private hands. All of this required the payment of government subsidies to most TOCs through OPRAF. Ironically, the total required to compensate the TOCs for the higher access charges was £1.6 billion in 1994/95, an increase of some 58% on the previous year, which was BR's last. With staffing and station costs still to be added, and the TOCs' only real income being from the fare-box, it was obvious that government support would be required by some franchises well into their franchise period, although ultimately the intention was that most operators would be paying a premium before their franchise ended.

Unlike the TOCs, Railtrack did not have to be successful in bidding for a franchise since it was effectively a licensed custodian owning its assets in perpetuity, provided it did not seriously breach its licence conditions. Even so, the costs of upgrading the West Coast Main Line would eventually bring about the fall of Railtrack, which was replaced by a new infrastructure custodian, Network Rail.

Getting ready for privatisation

Although the decision to privatise Britain's railways had been made, it was still necessary for British Rail to continue to manage the railway in the run-up to privatisation. BR also had a duty to prevent any deterioration in operations until the franchises were awarded, while at the same time beginning preparations for the handover to the successful bidders. Part of that preparatory work had seen British Rail reorganised, creating vertically integrated divisions, and the South West (SW) division, perhaps better known as Network SouthEast (which ultimately became the South West Trains franchise), was one of them.

Peter Field was the British Rail Divisional Director SW at the time, and he confirmed that between 1994 and 1996 the division effectively operated in shadow franchise form under the auspices of British Rail. Field added that the new British Rail SW division (which employed some 4,500 staff, of whom around 2,000 were traincrew) worked closely with the government to ensure the timetable for letting the franchise would be met, although at times it looked like being a close-run thing because there was no previous template to work to and it was imperative that the build-up to privatisation did not have a disruptive effect on the railway's day-to-day business. At the time it was known that the government looked favourably on bids from Management Buy Out (MBO) teams, and certainly the team assembled under Peter Field had that aspiration. Field recalled the difficulty in avoiding the obvious conflicts of interest that running the business, preparing it for sale and wanting to buy it posed, and told me that 'at times it was like walking a tightrope'. Equally important, Field told me, was 'the need to demonstrate the depth and strength of achievement if the SW division was to become a tasty crust for the private sector to gobble up'.

Field went on to say that 'arguably it was the best-constructed infrastructure on the railway and this had resulted in very high reliability'. The South West division had a huge commuter/leisure market (split approximately 60%/40%) and served some of the top 10 leisure destinations in the country. He also estimated that around one in eight Conservative MPs (the party in government at the time) lived along, or close to, its line of route, and a lot of politicians had a strong political drive to privatise the division quickly, the final process being described by some as the largest legal process in the history of Europe.

RIGHT: One of the tickets issued for the UK's first privatised train service, operated by SWT on 4 February 1996 – the 05:10 service from Twickenham to Waterloo. *John Balmforth*

Field also told me that in theory it would have been possible to split the South West division into around 11 micro-franchises, but they would have been very difficult to run. The government chose instead the option of breaking British Rail into 25 passenger rail franchises (together with some additional ones for freight), and ultimately South West Trains was selected to be one of the first three franchises to be let, the others being Great Western and LTS Rail (London, Tilbury & Southend). As things turned out, the South West Trains franchise was the first of the new franchises to be let and it also gained the accolade of operating the first passenger train to run following privatisation; the 05:10 Twickenham-London Waterloo on Sunday 4 February 1996, for which the company issued special souvenir tickets to mark the occasion.

CHAPTER THREE

1996: Stagecoach wins the South West Trains franchise

The government, through its Passenger Rail Franchise regulatory arm OPRAF, announced that the short-listed bidders for the South West Trains franchise would be:

- Sea Containers Ltd
- South West Trains Ltd (Stagecoach Holdings plc)
- Prism
- ASTIR (a Management Buy Out team led by Peter Field)

All were competing for the lucrative business rights to operate rail services across one of the UK's busiest rail networks stretching from the iconic London terminus at Waterloo to places as far afield as Basingstoke, Bournemouth, Brighton, Exeter, Penzance, Portsmouth, Salisbury, Southampton and Weymouth, as well as London's inner and outer south-western suburban routes. The franchise was also the biggest of the initial three to be offered to the private sector.

Prism withdrew its bid and eventually it became a two-horse race between Stagecoach and the Management Buy Out team's bid. A close-run race ultimately saw the Stagecoach bid triumphing by the narrow margin, in railway terms, of approximately £500,000. The winning bidder gained the rights to operate the franchise for a seven-year period and registered the name of the company as South West Trains Limited while operating as 'South West Trains'. As we shall see, a later successful bid to retain the franchise, albeit with the additional inclusion of the 'Island Line' franchise (previously operated by Stagecoach alongside its South West Trains franchise but with its own identity), effective from 4 February 2007, would see a change in the registered name of the company to Stagecoach South Western Trains Limited, but with the retention of the South West Trains operating name for its mainland services.

BELOW: The 10:48 Poole-Waterloo service approaches Southampton Central on 27 May 2004, formed of Class 442 'Wessex Electric' set No 2408 *County of Dorset. Brian Morrison*

TOP: SWT Class 458 set No 8012 stands alongside 'Desiro' Class 450 set No 450104 at Waterloo on 8 December 2007 as they await their next turn of duty. *Rich Mackin/railwayscene.co.uk*

MIDDLE: Newly refurbished SWT Class 455 set No 5715 is seen departing with a Waterloo to Waterloo via Richmond service on 1 September 2005. *Rich Mackin/railwayscene.co.uk*

BOTTOM: One of South West Trains' two-car Class 158/8 DMUs, set No 158889, makes a scheduled stop at Honiton. *South West Trains Picture Library*

In an in-depth interview Brian Souter gave refreshingly honest answers to questions that I posed. He had discovered that railways were unpopular with banks, telling me that 'NatWest would not even consider lending to anyone at the start of rail privatisation if the money was required to purchase a rail franchise'. Furthermore, many people were telling him that privatisation of the railway would be a disaster, but when he looked at the risks the main ones seemed to be:

- Unions – these had seemed vehemently opposed to privatising the UK's railways and British Rail did have a history of employee difficulties, but Souter said that 'Stagecoach had seen this before many times when taking over concerns within the bus industry and had generally developed good working relationships with its staff and unions'.
- Revenue – Stagecoach was used to managing revenue and Souter felt that Stagecoach had nothing to lose.
- The privatisation policy itself was politically unpopular to some.

Souter revealed that Stagecoach had good technical knowledge of the bus industry and a lot of business acumen. He also felt that while South West Trains had excellent technical knowledge and many really good managers (a view also held by Peter Field), with several of them going on to become big successes in their own right, the franchise needed business acumen injected into it. Souter admits that some of the Stagecoach board did have doubts, including his Finance Director, and that it was Souter himself who was pushing for the company to become involved in railways. However, the doubts were overcome and Souter was given 100% backing from the board when Stagecoach made its bid for the South West Trains franchise. Souter admitted he had looked at all three of the new franchises and had, in fact, also made an unsuccessful bid for the Great Western franchise. Nevertheless he had noted that South West Trains was the biggest and had many good attributes that he says are still there now, some 16 years later. He is convinced that they are the major reasons why the company survived the recession of the 1990s so well.

Souter recalled that Stagecoach was surprised to discover that it did not require a lot of money to purchase a rail franchise, the company just needing a big enough profit margin. The company decided that around 7% would be sufficient, and the franchise certainly had the potential to achieve that figure. However, both Peter Field, when heading the ASTIR (MBO) bid team, and Brian Souter admitted that they had struggled to understand the performance incentive regimes of Railtrack. There were two: one for the South West Trains franchise and another for the National network. Souter revealed to me that had Stagecoach fully understood the performance incentive regime, it might well not have won the franchise. Despite this he added that he was totally amazed to pay just £1 for the South West Trains franchise, then be handed a cheque for working capital of £48 million, although this did have to be repaid when the franchise ended. Souter explained that the working capital was high because South West Trains operated so many busy commuter services into London. He also accepts that the minimum Passenger Service Requirement in the early franchises, which set the target of trains arriving at their destinations on time at 87% of total mileage, was much easier to achieve than the 90%-plus in 2010 – a very different story. He also felt that the government would have preferred the first franchise to be let to have been to a Management Buy Out team in order to encourage others to bid for later franchises, a view also held by Field; interestingly, both the other franchises were let to MBO teams. Despite this, Souter said he found it to be a pretty positive experience running the franchise and admitted that economically Stagecoach got a very good deal.

Stagecoach also recognised the qualities found in the management team from British Rail days by retaining most in post, with Peter Field being appointed Managing Director, a position he held for some eight months before eventually leaving the company in September 1996 on friendly terms, having been headhunted on a number of occasions. Field was succeeded by the capable Brian Cox, who arrived from Stagecoach, and other notable Managing Directors in Andrew Haines (twice), Graham Eccles, Stewart Palmer and, from October 2009, Andy Pitt.

Waterloo station

Although Waterloo station is owned and managed by Network Rail, it is the London terminal used by South West Trains for its services (although it makes significant use of interchanges at Clapham Junction and Vauxhall), and its importance to the TOC must not be underestimated as evidenced by the 100,000-plus passengers using the station every weekday during the 3 hours of the morning peak.

The Waterloo station known to so many of today's rail users – the UK's largest main-line rail station, covering an area totalling 24½ acres

BELOW: This superb aerial photo of South West Trains' London terminus at Waterloo shows two SWT 'Desiro' Class 450 sets passing on the complex layout at the station approach, as well as the disused former Eurostar terminal to the immediate right of the station. The Victory Arch commemorating the LSWR staff who lost their lives in the First World War is seen at the bottom right, while the railway line in the foreground is the through line between Waterloo East and Charing Cross. *Phil Metcalfe*

– is the result of a gradual sequence of change, mostly in its early life. In view of this it is worth taking a brief chronological look at it here:

- The original station was opened on 11 July 1848 by the London & South Western Railway (LSWR)
- A connection to the South Eastern Railway was opened in January 1864, surviving until decommissioning on 26 March 1911
- The Necropolis station opened in October 1854, replaced by a new station in November 1885
- The North station opened on 3 August 1860, receiving an additional platform in November 1885
- Waterloo Junction station, today's Waterloo East, opened on 1 January 1869
- The South station opened on 15 December 1878

ABOVE: A familiar sight for many using Waterloo is the famous concourse clock, which over the years has been used by so many people as a convenient meeting place, the need for which is obvious at such a busy station. *John Balmforth*

RIGHT: A variety of unit types can be seen in this very busy scene during the early days of the newly won South West Trains franchise. A Eurostar train can just be seen at the bottom left of the picture. *South West Trains Picture Library*

LEFT: Waterloo station is seen just after the morning peak on 3 April 2009. The large number of trains present is evidence of the busy commuter service provided by SWT. The bodies of the 'Desiro' units can be fitted to trains using third rail or overhead line power supplies. The SWT versions operate on third rail 750V dc current, but the depression in the roof styling to accommodate a pantograph is clearly seen. *John Balmforth*

- The Waterloo & City Line station opened on 8 August 1898
- The station was completely rebuilt between 1900 and 1922 and officially reopened on 21 March 1922
- The roof and platforms of the 1922 station were designed by J. W. Jacomb-Hood and A. W. Szlumper, engineers for the LSWR. The roof is of transverse ridge and furrow construction measuring 520 by 540ft, with a maximum single span of 118ft. The station's office buildings were designed by J. R. Scott, the chief architect for the LSWR. Of Imperial Baroque style, they are notable for the Victory Arch, constructed of Portland stone, which commemorates the loss of railway servicemen in the First World War and carries statues depicting war and peace located below a statue of Britannia
- The Necropolis station was bombed during the Second World War on 16 April 1941 and was never rebuilt
- The concourse as it appears today underwent remodelling work between 1978 and 1983
- The inaugural Eurostar service from Waterloo International ran on 14 November 1994
- In 2008 the International section of the station previously used by Eurostar for through services to France and Belgium was closed after that operator transferred its London terminus across the city to St Pancras. Since then all of the station's main-line rail services have been provided by South West Trains

In a statement of changes required to Network Rail's latest delivery plan for enhancements to the UK rail network released during 2009, the Office of Rail Regulation (ORR) stated that it expects the conversion of the former Waterloo International Terminal for use by domestic services to be completed by the December 2011 timetable change. The work will include an additional signal section as well as the moving of buffer stops to create a large level concourse, though this will be completed ahead of any other works at the station.

Initial problems: shortage of drivers and troublesome trains!

Despite Brian Souter's assertion that Stagecoach and the British Rail South West division had between them a wealth of management experience, he readily admits that the franchise could not have got off to a worse start as Stagecoach found that railways were a different kettle of fish when compared to the bus industry. Souter explained that Stagecoach had a policy of reviewing resources after purchasing new companies in order to get stability and consistency right across the board, and when it was awarded the South West Trains franchise the company commenced the usual resource review. The completed review concluded that the drivers' roster showed a poor use of resources and suggested that the company had too many drivers. This resulted in many drivers being allowed to leave on generous redundancy packages, and Peter Field recalled that initially it meant 'getting rid of a lot of staff and

RIGHT: Staff undergoing training at the South West Trains Operations and Safety Training Centre, Basingstoke, using its wonderfully named fictional location 'Wittsend Junction'. *South West Trains Picture Library*

restructuring terms and conditions of drivers and guards'. He told me that although the package offered to staff was a good one, the company did let too many drivers go.

For a short period SWT was not sure how many drivers it would need and consequently held off recruiting trainee drivers. In fact, it eventually emerged that driver numbers was not really the major issue, but rather it was that of driver route knowledge. It is not simply a case of the signallers setting points and signals for drivers to follow. In-depth knowledge is required of the route itself – braking points, speed limits and station locations, to identify just a few items, as well as significant traction knowledge enabling drivers to identify and remedy any faults that develop. As we shall see, driver training is intensive and the standard of applicants high. Souter also admits that he had misjudged the time it took to train new drivers and agreed that he had failed to understand rail-specific issues such as rest day working. The outcome was a large number of trains being cancelled, which attracted bad publicity in the media, some of which the new franchise owner felt was a little harsh. Souter said 'the number of cancellations had been no worse than had sometimes been the case under British Rail's stewardship'.

BELOW: The emergency services regularly stage major rail incident practices. In this scene Fire, Police, Ambulance and Rail staff can be seen using Class 455 and 319 sets to enact a major incident on the railway, ensuring their readiness should a real-life incident occur. *South West Trains Picture Library*

Staff training

Stewart Palmer (Managing Director of SWT, 2006-2009) told me that he is extremely proud of the purpose-built Operations and Safety Training Centre located close to Basingstoke station, where the training of all staff is undertaken. He added that the centre has very high-quality trainers and the 2009 economic downturn has not seen any cutback in essential training needs, especially those that are safety critical. He did admit that the provision of first aid training was no longer seen as essential for all front-line staff and, where it is provided, the company has to ensure that facilities can be made available for staff to attend courses to renew their certificates on a regular basis, which is a costly exercise. It is instead restricted to appropriate staff at key stations, and some of these are also trained in the use of defibrillators.

The training centre is superbly equipped to enable high-quality training to be provided, thus supplying the company with extremely professional and competent personnel. Palmer told me that on average, for staff to complete training and enter revenue-earning service, it takes around

- 15 months for drivers
- 6 weeks for guards
- 4/5 weeks for other staff.

Additionally South West Trains still offers apprenticeships on the engineering side of its business.

I visited the training centre in July 2009 and saw at first hand the excellent facilities available, including a section called 'Centre Stage', which contains the wonderfully named 'Wittsend Junction' station mock-up, where professional actors are often engaged to play the roles of passengers. Trainees find themselves faced with just about any scenario they are likely to meet in their day-to-day contact with passengers during their railway careers. Led by the then Managing Director, Andrew Haines, this proved to be the beginning of a culture change in staff training at South West Trains.

The company also purchased four driver training simulators from Munich-based German company Kraus-Maffei Wegmann in 2002 at a cost of £1.3 million. At first glance this may seem a huge investment for a Train Operating Company with a comparatively short-life franchise, but the use of the simulators resulted in a huge leap in driver training standards. Previously a trainee driver could only gain his traction experience by being out and about driving under supervision, it being perfectly possible (and frequently so) to complete training without experiencing anything out of the ordinary. The simulators have changed all that and instructors can now set a trainee driver just about any situation to deal with. On top of this they are used for the rules examinations that all drivers have to undergo periodically, thus ensuring consistent standards right across the company.

Applications for driver positions are always heavily oversubscribed, resulting in disappointment for many, but this does allow South West Trains to 'raise the bar' in terms of the standards of the people it employs. Applicants come from all sorts of backgrounds; I visited a class of trainees in the fourth week of their training course that included a former accountant and a former bus driver.

As is rightly expected, the training courses are exacting and testing, not only at South West Trains but right across the rail industry. This is clearly illustrated by the current South West Trains driver training syllabus, reproduced in Appendix A with the kind consent of the South West Trains Operations and Safety Training Centre at Basingstoke.

LEFT: An interesting aerial view of Basingstoke station during the major infrastructure remodelling recently undertaken at the London end of the station. The line diverging off to the left in the top right of the picture is the route to Reading. *South West Trains Picture Library*

ABOVE: A driver's-eye view from Class 159/1 set No 159105 travelling along the Down Main, as 'Desiro' Class 444 set No 444031 passes Battersea flyover travelling in the opposite direction on its way to Waterloo. *John Balmforth*

MIDDLE: Complex points and crossings have to be negotiated to gain access to Waterloo station. South West Trains Class 455, 159 and 458 sets are seen in the background. *John Balmforth*

BOTTOM: The approach to the London end of Basingstoke station as seen from the cab of Class 159/1 set No 159105 on 3 July 2009, forming the 09:50 service from Waterloo to Salisbury. *John Balmforth*

TOP: The driver's-eye view of Wimbledon from the cab of SWT Class 159 set No 159105 as it approaches with the Salisbury service from Waterloo. *John Balmforth*

MIDDLE: Taken from the cab on the same day, this scene just south of Woking station sees SWT 'Desiro' Class 444 set No 444015 passing on its way to Waterloo. *John Balmforth*

BELOW: Another driver's-eye view from the cab of No 159105 as it passes through Berrylands station at speed on the Down Fast line, looking towards Surbiton. Approaching on the Up Fast is an SWT Class 159 set, while on the Down Slow about to be overtaken is a Class 455 set. *John Balmforth*

Once the company had overcome the initial driver shortage issues, the fledgling operator then faced another early challenge when its Class 442 'Wessex Electric' trainsets started to develop hot axle boxes. Peter Field explained that this resulted in the entire fleet being withdrawn temporarily on safety grounds, leading, perhaps unfairly, to yet more bad publicity. A detailed investigation into the issue showed that the problem had been caused by grease contamination, an issue for which South West Trains was, perhaps again unfairly, fined £1 million – a matter that still annoys Brian Souter to this day.

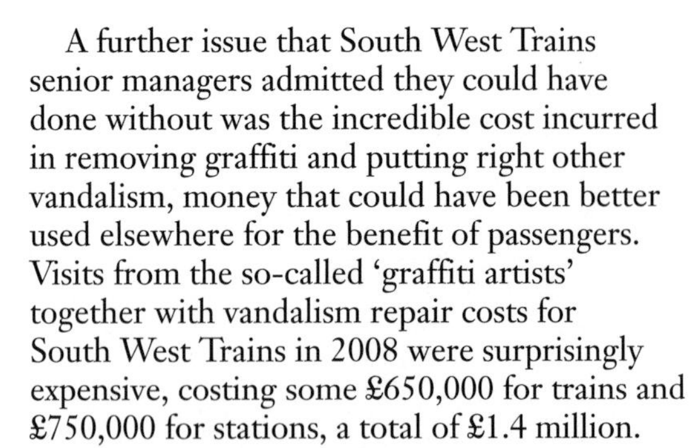

A further issue that South West Trains senior managers admitted they could have done without was the incredible cost incurred in removing graffiti and putting right other vandalism, money that could have been better used elsewhere for the benefit of passengers. Visits from the so-called 'graffiti artists' together with vandalism repair costs for South West Trains in 2008 were surprisingly expensive, costing some £650,000 for trains and £750,000 for stations, a total of £1.4 million.

Much of the cost is labour, as the cleaning-up work is very labour intensive. Not only do these so-called 'artists' cause damage and disruption to train services while trains are out of use being repaired, but they also put their own and others' lives at risk.

BELOW: Before its gangway connection was revised to all-yellow, No 2416 *Mum in a Million – Doreen Scanlon*, the first Class 442 'Wessex Electric' set to be modified and painted into South West Trains livery, stands inside Crewe Works after the completion of its micro-refurbishment on 6 March 1998. *Brian Morrison*

Innovation – a number of 'firsts'

Despite the early difficulties it faced, South West Trains continued to make progress, including the achievement of a number of 'firsts' in the UK rail industry. These included:

- The introduction of a passenger panel through which passengers regularly meet with senior management. This was soon followed by its 'Travelsafe' scheme, which provided uniformed staff specially trained by the British Transport Police (BTP), but funded by South West Trains, with a mandate to provide reassurance to passengers. The successful scheme was the forerunner of today's Rail Community Officers, whose training is again provided by the BTP and funded by the Train Operating Company.
- The development of an Integrated Control Centre with dedicated CCTV. Located at Wimbledon, it sees South West Trains, Network Rail and maintenance managers all working side by side and has now been emulated by many other operators UK-wide.

BELOW LEFT: The annoying results of a visit from the 'graffiti artist' can be seen on the carriage side of 'Desiro' Class 450 set No 450018. The cost to SWT is immense in terms of the loss of the train from service and the actual cost of putting right the damage. *South West Trains Picture Library*

BELOW RIGHT: So-called 'graffiti artists' are the bane of modern-day life and the railway has not escaped their attention. It costs the railway vast sums of money to clean up after they have paid a visit, as well as putting trains out of service. This is an example of damage done to an Island Line Class 483 unit. With only six two-car sets available, Island Line can ill afford to have one out of use. *South West Trains Picture Library*

LEFT: A busy scene on Platform 3a at Southampton Central sees passengers boarding one of SWT's diesel multiple-units, Class 158 set No 158880, as it makes a station stop on its way to Salisbury in April 2009. *John Balmforth*

December 2004 saw the complete rewrite of the South West Trains timetable – another first for a TOC following privatisation – requiring some 1,700 trains to be retimed.

The previous major timetable change covering the franchise's route network had been introduced in 1967 when the Waterloo to Bournemouth main line was electrified. Since that time the number of passengers had increased dramatically, passenger flows had altered – for example, people had begun commuting greater distances into London – and the timetable had gradually become more complicated as a result of trying to cope with all the changing demands being placed upon it. The December 2004 timetable rewrite was tasked with achieving a number of things by attempting to standardise and simplify it as much as possible. It successfully achieved:

- The same timetable and calling pattern of trains hour after hour throughout the day during Monday to Saturday
- All main suburban trains calling at all stations between Waterloo and Wimbledon
- All stopping services on the Windsor lines calling at all stations between Waterloo and Barnes
- A reduction in the number of crossing moves between running lines
- Stock and train crews limited as far as possible to the same routes during the day in order to prevent delays transferring from one route to another
- As few additional stops as possible during the peaks.

The degree of difficulty in achieving a successful outcome to this major project, effectively starting again with a blank sheet of paper, must not be underestimated as, together with some increased station dwell times, it resulted in fewer decisions having to be made on regulating trains, as well as improving punctuality.

South West Trains has also consistently scored highly in the independent National Passenger Surveys – a record of which the company is rightly proud. The quality performance levels resulted in the TOC winning the ACoRP overall 'Rail Operator of the Year' award in 2005, recognised as being especially difficult for a commuter operator to achieve.

BELOW: The gleaming paintwork of newly delivered SWT 'Turbostar' Class170 set No 170301 is a stark contrast to the weather as it awaits its next turn of duty at Salisbury in October 2003. *South West Trains Picture Library*

ABOVE: Making station stops at Basingstoke's Platforms 1 and 2 respectively are SWT 'Desiro' Class 444 set No 444022 on its way to Poole, and Class 159 set No 159009 heading for the West Country. *John Balmforth*

RIGHT: An SWT Class 444 set empties its full load of commuters onto Waterloo's Platform 7 during the morning rush hour. The curved platforms require the use of 'Banner Repeater' signals to warn staff with a restricted view along the platforms that the main signal aspect may not be clear. In this view both 'Banner Repeaters' indicate that their parent signals are set at red. *Stagecoach Group Picture Library*

CHAPTER FOUR

The franchise is extended

With the franchise due to end in February 2003, the Shadow Strategic Rail Authority (sSRA) issued a press release dated 17 August 2000 that revealed three companies shortlisted to bid for the franchise:

- Stagecoach Holdings plc (franchisee of South West Trains and Island Line)
- First Group plc (franchisee of Great Eastern, Great Western and North Western) in association with Nederlandse Spoorwegen (Dutch Railways)
- GNER Holdings Limited (subsidiary of Sea Containers Ltd and franchisee of GNER)

In the press release, Mike Grant, sSRA Chief Executive, described the franchise thus:

'The South West Trains franchisee is a significant operator in the rail network, with many thousands of commuters depending on its services for their daily journey to work. Replacement of this franchise is a prerequisite to providing relief to the current pressure that exists on capacity in the approach to Waterloo. The decision to shortlist these three companies follows careful consideration of the proposals we received. We shall now be embarking on negotiations to decide the future owner of this franchise. Throughout this process our key aim will be to ensure the best possible deal for the passenger, with strong investment commitments and improved customer service, along with value for the taxpayer.'

RIGHT: The final official slam-door service at Waterloo on 25 May 2005, the 11:35 to Bournemouth, poses with its carriage doors open. The benefit to operating staff from the withdrawal of this type of stock is obvious as well as the improvement to passenger safety.
Brian Morrison

TOP LEFT: All four tracks in Clapham cutting to and from Waterloo are occupied by SWT trains on 28 July 2005, with two Class 455/8 sets heading for Guildford via Epsom, and Dorking to Waterloo via Epsom respectively, a Class 159 set forming a Waterloo to Salisbury service, and a Class 450 'Desiro' set en route to Waterloo from Alton. The sets are Nos 5861, 5867, 159006 and 450011 respectively. *Brian Morrison*

TOP RIGHT: South West Trains local services from Woking to Waterloo and from Waterloo to Shepperton pass near Wimbledon on 12 February 2008, formed of Class 455/8s. Set No 5860 is the rear unit of the Woking train and the Shepperton-bound service is formed of Nos 5871 and 5852. *Brian Morrison*

RIGHT: Still wearing the British Rail Network SouthEast livery, Class 455/9 set No 5913 passes Kew Junction on 21 April 1996 while working a service from Waterloo to Windsor & Eton. *Brian Morrison*

However, the franchise was never put out to tender; instead the Strategic Rail Authority announced that it had developed a new way forward to 2007 for the South West Trains franchise. The plan provided for a one-year extension to the existing Stagecoach-owned franchise, taking it up to February 2004, together with an agreement of key principles with Stagecoach Holdings plc for a new franchise that would run on to February 2007. These included:

- Replacement of Mark 1 (slam-door) trains
- A new performance plan
- The introduction of additional Sunday and evening services
- Completion of design studies for extending suburban platforms to increase capacity.

SRA chairman Richard Bowker explained:

'This agreement allows South West Trains to focus on what matters to passengers – recovering performance to a level that passengers deserve and expect and the replacement of slam-door trains with the biggest new train order in the UK. Taken together these will help to deliver a better, more reliable service for its passengers, which is the ultimate goal for any Train Operating Company.'

At the same time the SRA revealed its intention for all domestic services into Waterloo to be operated by South West Trains as part of its objective of having a single operator at each main London terminus.

On 11 July 2003 the Strategic Rail Authority announced that it had signed a new three-year franchise with the incumbent Stagecoach Group plc to operate South West Trains until 2007. The three-year franchise deal required a major commitment from South West Trains, and Brian Souter is delighted that the company achieved them all. They included:

- Continued implementation of a detailed performance plan to improve punctuality and reliability
- Delivery into service of new 'Desiro' carriages over the next two years to replace the existing 576 slam-door carriages, which to this day remains one of Brian Souter's most memorable achievements. The deal also underpinned the financing of the new depots necessary for the new trains, including the brand-new purpose-built Northam Depot.
- Continued investment in CCTV at stations, an improved train cleaning regime and an accelerated station repainting programme
- Overhaul and refurbishment of the Class 455 metro carriages to improve reliability and passenger comfort
- The continuation of service improvements – some longer peak-hour trains and improved Sunday and late-night frequencies, which had been introduced as part of the earlier one-year extension to the franchise.

The attainment of such exacting requirements should not be underestimated. It certainly showed the company's huge commitment to the rail industry.

CHAPTER **FIVE**

Northam Traincare Depot

RIGHT: One of South West Trains' 'Desiro' sets has its wheels returned to 'as new' condition during a visit to the wheel-turning lathe at Northam. *J. A. Morgan, South West Trains*

BOTTOM: The ultra-modern depot facilities at Northam include this wheel-turning lathe, which, in addition to re-turning damaged wheels, sees trains visit at specific intervals: 112,000 miles for motor coaches and 240,000 for trailer coaches. *John Balmforth*

All Train Operating Companies require high-quality maintenance facilities in order to keep their fleets in a good and safe working order. South West Trains services operate over a wide route area and it is necessary for the company to provide accessible maintenance and stabling facilities at a number of different locations; these are listed in Appendix E.

The work carried out at the main facilities varies from simply stabling trainsets through to cleaning, carriage washing and refuelling to full-blown maintenance. Their importance cannot be underestimated, so it is worth taking a look behind the scenes at the company's newest Traincare Depot (TCD), Northam at Southampton, the development of which is itself an interesting story.

The new purpose-built facility was dedicated to the maintenance of the 'Desiro' Class 444 and 450 trainsets. The Siemens day-to-day maintenance contract for the new trains was with South West Trains, but because franchises

TOP: For safety purposes trains cannot be driven onto the wheel lathe under their own power, so a specially purchased battery-operated shunter is used. Here 'Desiro' No 450544, with High Capacity seating layout, is seen being shunted into the workshop. *John Balmforth*

ABOVE: Among the excellent equipment in use at Northam TCD is this bogie drop facility. Bogies are lowered and removed to a workshop area via the underground exit seen at the left-hand side of the picture. *John Balmforth*

do sometimes change hands it included a facility to roll over the contract to a new franchisee if required. The contract, which included the cost of building the new Northam TCD, runs for 25 years with a start contract value of £1.3 billion and covers 733 coaches.

However, first a suitable location had to be found. It had to be near the main line and somewhere central to the South West Trains network of routes. Several locations were looked at, including Fratton, but it was discovered that the land next to the existing depot had already been sold. Another depot still in use from BR days was at Eastleigh. This in fact satisfied the requirements, but it was still in use by the English Welsh & Scottish Railway Company and consequently was not available. However, a site at Northam, Southampton (not very far from Eastleigh), was found, which furthermore could provide direct access to the main running lines. With the location chosen, the green light was given for a deal to be signed between South West Trains, Siemens and Angel Trains, allowing construction work to commence in October 2001 at an estimated cost of £26 million. It was subsequently discovered that it would be necessary to incorporate a new power sub-station to provide sufficient electricity supplies to operate the new trains, increasing the cost to £33.5 million. Network Rail had anticipated that the work would take around three years to complete, but the project constructors, Fitzpatrick and Birse, completed the work in January 2003, some 22 months ahead of schedule. The depot was the first of its type to be constructed for some 30 years, and included a 6,415m^2 four-road carriage shed.

The Northam Traincare facility is capable of holding 22 'Desiro' four/five-car trainsets, and has its own 750V dc sub-station to provide traction power supply. Successful completion of commissioning trials for the new trains enabled the depot to go 'live' in September 2003, and into full revenue-earning service in October of the same year.

The maintenance philosophy adopted was seen as critical to the success of the new fleet and it was essential that:

- availability be determined by operational needs and not engineering requirements – a target of 100% availability being set for peak-period operation
- the modular design of equipment be integrated into the maintenance regime.
- vehicle design had to be 'maintenance friendly'
- maintenance activities must enhance vehicle and system reliability
- maintenance facilities must assist in minimising vehicle downtime
- staff skills profiles must maximise operational flexibility.

Steve Walker, Siemens' Fleet Director, and Eddie Milligan, Siemens' Production Services Manager at Northam, explained that the technology used on the 'Desiro' sets was totally new, with both the Class 444 and 450 sets being able to 'talk' to the depot electronically even when the trains were miles away from it, allowing problem-solving to be carried out remotely. They added that this required a culture change for both the trains' drivers and the maintenance teams because it was so different from what had happened in the past. Some of the depot staff well grounded in the old rolling stock initially had to look after both the 'old' and the 'new', and needed to accept the new technology. They did so, and Milligan told me that without the culture change the introduction of the new trains into revenue-earning service could have been delayed.

TOP: A view of the reception sidings at the joint Siemens/SWT maintenance depot at Northam near Southampton, with two 12-car 'Desiro' Class 450 sets accompanied by a lone Class 444 set. The depression in the roof profile allows for the fitting of a pantograph for trains equipped to operate over routes with a 25,000kV overhead line power supply. *John Balmforth*

MIDDLE: 'Desiro' Class 444 and 450 sets Nos 444005 and 450111 stand on the arrivals road at the depot on 20 April 2009. *John Balmforth*

BOTTOM: 'Desiro' Class 444 sets Nos 444010 and 444025 are caught by the camera awaiting attention at Northam TCD in April 2009. *John Balmforth*

ABOVE: 'Desiro' Class 450 sets Nos 450072 and 450029 are seen in company with an unidentified sister set undergoing routine maintenance inside Northam depot on 20 April 2009.
John Balmforth

MIDDLE: Viewed from the upper gantry inside Northam TCD in April 2009 are 'Desiro' outer-suburban sets Nos 450072, 450124 and 450029.
John Balmforth

BOTTOM: 'Desiro' Class 450 and 444 sets Nos 450012 and 444010 await attention at Northam depot. The bogie drop and its controls are clearly visible in the foreground.
John Balmforth

He added that 60% of Northam TCD's workforce were new to the industry, so they had no cultural gap to bridge; many are ex-forces personnel, and both morale and results are superb. Milligan went on to say that the teamwork between the 'old hands' and new staff is superb and he is especially proud of all concerned.

Northam TCD has a 228-strong workforce (excluding cleaning staff) trained to different abilities and needs. In order to achieve top-grade status, technicians receive 30 weeks of training spread over a two-to-three-year period. Training courses are rotated around the company's training facilities, but approximately 75% are carried out on site at Northam. Eddie Milligan said that 'the depot has a very low turnover of staff with a high degree of job satisfaction'. In a reference to the quality of his technicians, he told me that he was not surprised, because if a man can look after the maintenance of RAF jets during the war in the Middle East, he could certainly adapt to the new technology carried by the new trains.

Some faults need to be referred and redesigned to prevent constant failing. Northam has a special team to do this, giving an ability to identify both actual and potential issues. 'Level Checks' have been written to identify the level of check required; for example, there may be no need to pull a train apart if it is the first time a fault has occurred, but on the third occurrence of a fault its entire system is checked. The big advantage of written level checks is continuity. When a shift ends, the incoming shift will simply take up the investigation from the point reached, instead of starting all over again. New diagnostic test equipment is also being developed at Northam so that actual problems can be identified, not just with the electrics.

TOP: 'Desiro' Class 450 set No 450029 undergoes routine maintenance at Northam TCD in April 2009. The pleasant, clean working conditions are a big step-change from those experienced in the depots of BR days. *John Balmforth*

BOTTOM LEFT: Class 444 'Desiro' set No 444028 arrives at Bournemouth on 25 February 2008, forming the 12:39 from Waterloo to Poole. *Brian Morrison*

BOTTOM RIGHT: Class 450 'Desiro' set No 450013 departs from Weymouth on 11 January 2004 and climbs to Bincombe summit with a service for Waterloo. *Brian Morrison*

ABOVE SWT's white main-line livery really suits the 'Desiro' body style, as can be seen in this shot of Class 444 set No 444008 passing Northam en route to Waterloo. *John Balmforth*

A good example is the trains' couplers. Eddie Milligan pointed out that the equipment examines the integrity of connection, but that diagnostics cannot do that – you need good old-fashioned maintenance skills.

As in most railway depots, much of the work is carried out at night when the trains finish service for the day. Four trainsets are retained at Northam every 24 hours for examinations, all levels of train examination being undertaken. As befits its status as a purpose-built Traincare Facility, Northam boasts:

- a wheel drop facility
- a double-headed remote-shunted wheel-turning lathe
- a carriage-washing plant that will operate at temperatures down to -5°C
- stabling with controlled emission toilet-emptying facilities
- electronic train monitoring and depot security systems.

Siemens' service contract with South West Trains at its Northam Traincare Depot provides the TOC with:

- vehicle maintenance
- interior and exterior cleaning (sets are washed on every visit to Northam TCD)
- servicing
- daily train preparation
- provision of rolling stock maintenance control
- daily allocation of trainsets to operate diagrams
- full technical support for the vehicles.

Minimum levels of trainset availability to ensure that SWT's service levels can be maintained are:

- Class 444: 45 sets, of which 42 are required daily
- Class 450: 28 High Capacity (HC) sets, of which 26 are required daily
- Class 450: 99 non-HC sets, of which 91 are required daily.

A total of 22 'Desiro' sets are stabled at Northam every night, but all are required to return for regular maintenance as follows:

- Class 444: every 20 days (16,000 miles)
- Class 450: every 28 days (16,000 miles).

The 'Desiro' sets also return for attention on the wheel-turning lathe:

- Motor coaches: every 112,000 miles
- Trailer coaches: every 240,000 miles.

Siemens had always intended to improve its relationships with contractual partners, which had sometimes been adversarial. In this respect Northam TCD is a trailblazer and Siemens works very closely with South West Trains, having built an excellent relationship. Communications workshops are held, giving respective managers the means of resolving issues, and SWT has its own desk at Northam.

LEFT: South West Trains 'Desiro' set No 444026 is seen at Southampton Central's busy Platform 4 while forming a Bournemouth-Waterloo service on 3 April 2009. *John Balmforth*

CHAPTER SIX

2007: Stagecoach retains the South Western Trains franchise

When the initial South West Trains franchise won by Stagecoach in 1996 (subsequently extended firstly for 12 months and again for a further three-year period) neared its completion, the Department for Transport (DfT) announced that it would be re-let with effect from 4 February 2007 and would be a combination of the existing South West Trains and Island Line franchises for a period of 10 years. Both franchises had previously been operated by Stagecoach but with their own independent boards of directors and separate identities. On 20 December 2005 the DfT announced that the five pre-qualified bidders were:

- Stagecoach South Western Trains Ltd
- First South Western Ltd (FirstGroup plc)
- Great South Western Railway Company Ltd (a joint venture between GNER Holdings Ltd and MTR Corporation Ltd of Hong Kong)
- Arriva Trains South West Ltd (Arriva plc)
- Trafalgar Trains Ltd (National Express Group).

All were invited by the DfT to submit detailed bids for the South Western franchise.

The successful bidder, registered in London as 'Stagecoach South Western Trains Ltd', gained the right to run the UK's busiest commuter rail franchise. Still known to most passengers simply as 'South West Trains', the company is a wholly owned subsidiary of Stagecoach Group, which, as we have already seen, is one of the UK's biggest public transport operators. As its name suggests, South West Trains operates passenger rail services in South West England with the majority of its trains operating on 750V dc

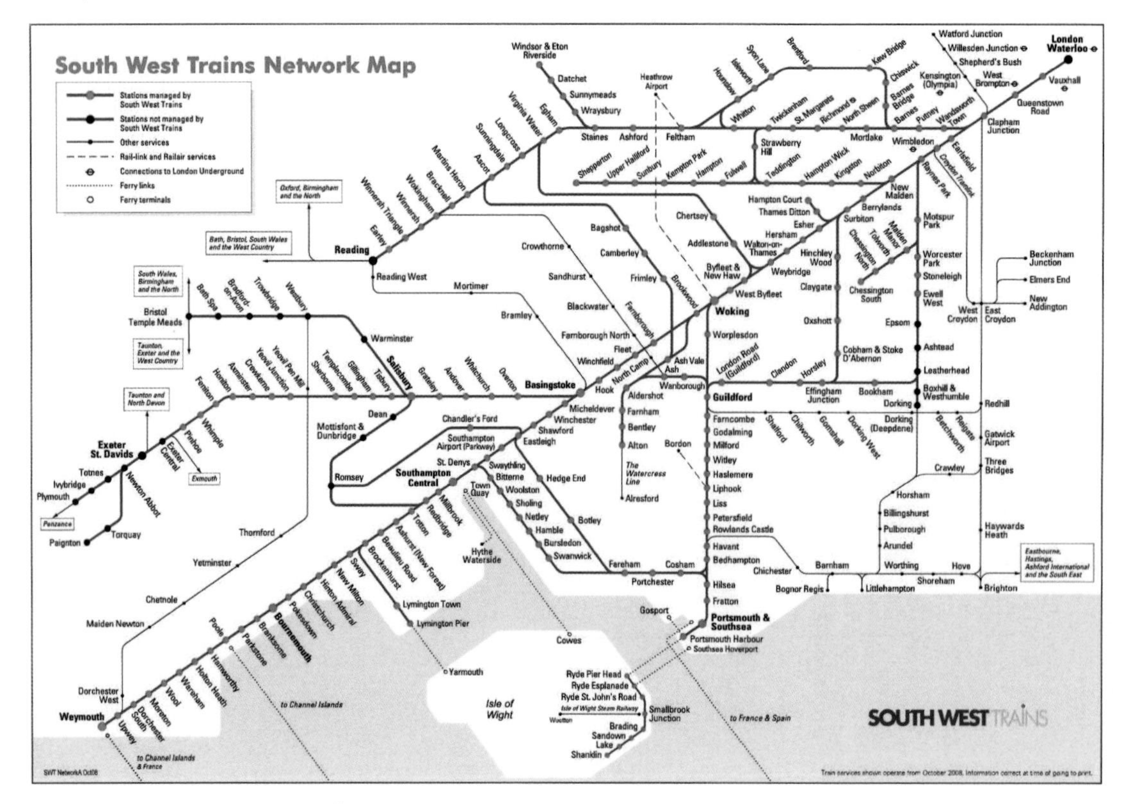

LEFT: South West Trains route network map. *South West Trains*

third rail power supply, but with a small diesel fleet for use on services to the West of England. Its routes contain the largest commuter rail network in the UK and are centred on London's Waterloo station, the train operator running some 1,650 trains a day carrying around 162 million passengers per year. The routes are best described as follows:

The six main-line routes

1. South Western Main Line serving Southampton Central, Bournemouth, Poole and Weymouth
2. Portsmouth Direct Line via Guildford and Haslemere
3. West of England Main Line serving Exeter, Paignton, Plymouth and Penzance (SWT services west of Exeter St David's ended in December 2009 in accordance with the terms of the SWT franchise)
4. Wessex Main Line – Southampton Central-Bristol Temple Meads via Salisbury
5. London Waterloo-Portsmouth Harbour via Basingstoke and Eastleigh
6. London Waterloo-Reading via Staines and Ascot

ABOVE: The official launch of the Penzance-Waterloo service – a joint operation between Wales & West and South West Trains – took place on 28 September 2000. SWT Class 159 set No 159016 was used to form the 14:25 departure for Waterloo. *Colin J. Marsden*

BELOW: Passing heavy seas, SWT Class 159 set No 159015 traverses the Up line at Dawlish as the 17:47 Plymouth-Waterloo service on 21 September 2006. *Colin J. Marsden*

ABOVE: SWT Class 158 DMU set No 158889 is caught at Weymouth's Platform 1 before commencing a Network Rail foliage-checking trip. *Nigel Trower, South West Trains*

ABOVE RIGHT: Forming the 17:49 South West Trains service from Plymouth to London Waterloo, Class 159 set No 159022 descends Rattery Bank towards Totnes on 7 April 2008. *Brian Morrison*

RIGHT: South West Trains Class 455/8 set No 5858 snowbound at Epsom in February 2009, displaying the rather obvious 'Not In Service' on its destination blind. *Peter Bumstead, South West Trains*

The six suburban route groups

1 Waterloo-Reading from Clapham Junction
Hounslow Loop Line from Barnes to Whitton or Feltham
Windsor branch from Staines
Chertsey Loop Line from Virginia Water to Weybridge
Ascot-Ash Vale via Camberley
2 Mole Valley Line from Raynes Park to Dorking via Epsom
Chessington branch from Motspur Park
Guildford-Leatherhead branch
3 Kingston Loop Line, from New Malden (Main Line) to Twickenham (Reading Line)
Shepperton branch from Teddington via New Malden or Twickenham
4 New Guildford Line
Surbiton-Guildford via Cobham
Guildford-London via Woking or Camberley
5 Hampton Court branch from Surbiton
6 Alton branch from Brookwood

The other routes

1 Southampton local lines
Salisbury-Romsey via Southampton Central and Chandlers Ford (service to Totton now discontinued)
2 Lymington branch
Brockenhurst-Lymington Pier (for ferry services to the Isle of Wight)

TOP: One of South West Trains' inner-suburban Class 455/7 sets, No 5725, pauses at Wimbledon Park en route to Shepperton via Kingston when working route 24. *South West Trains Picture Library*

BELOW: With the Stagecoach orange stripes added to the Network SouthEast livery, Class 455/7 set No 5714 awaits departure time at Waterloo on 29 November 1996, forming the 16:31 service for Epsom. *Brian Morrison*

BOTTOM: Two of South West Trains' Class 455 inner-suburban sets stand side by side at Waterloo in April 2009. Visible in the background is an SWT Class 159 set. *John Balmforth*

The effect of the 2008/09 recession on South West Trains

It is fair to say that the early years of the new franchise have not been without their difficulties. Initially performance and reliability continued to be good, making South West Trains one of the UK's top rail franchises, the TOC regularly rating highly in the independently produced National Rail Trends reports. Everything appeared to suggest that the high premium payments due to the government under the new franchise were both justified and sustainable, although as we shall see they have been questioned by some commentators. One certainty, however, is that the company could not have foreseen the dramatic effects that the economic recession of 2009 would bring.

Stagecoach Chief Executive Brian Souter, referring to the parent company's preliminary results in April 2009, said: 'While our rail operations are more sensitive to the macro-economic cycle, we have acted quickly to protect our businesses. We have delivered a major cost-reduction programme at our rail franchises and we are implementing measures to protect passenger revenue and attract new customers to the rail network.' The cost-cutting programme inevitably included a reduction in the size of the workforce, and early in 2009 the company announced plans to reduce this by around 10%. The planned cuts included:

- 25 management staff
- 14 clerical staff
- 93 full-time ticket office staff
- 87 part-time ticket office staff
- 62 full-time platform staff.

Some of the potential cuts put South West Trains on a head-on collision course with the Rail Maritime & Transport union, which reacted furiously, one of its officials pointing out that fares had gone up and company profits were up 7.6% the previous year, at £59 million. South West Trains responded that 'we are proposing to reduce the costs of our rail operation and make some changes to the way we manage our business. Taking into account existing vacancies and posts which have been withdrawn, this will mean that the actual number of people leaving will be around 200.' When I interviewed him, Brian Souter confirmed this and added that 'most of the job losses will be achieved by voluntary redundancy and natural wastage. I expect very few redundancies and confirm there will be no reduction in driver or guard staffing levels.'

ABOVE: South West Trains' green-painted heritage stock, Class 421 '3-CIG' set No 1498, stands at Brockenhurst station's Platform 4a on 1 September 2005, ready to form the shuttle service to Lymington Pier for ferry connections to the Isle of Wight. *Rich Mackin/ railwayscene.co.uk*

RIGHT: Class 421/7 '3-CIG' No 1499 at Lymington Pier on 12 May 2005, awaiting departure time as the branch shuttle to Brockenhurst. *Brian Morrison*

LEFT: Class 421/4 No 1885 is seen en route to Bournemouth Traincare Depot working as Empty Coaching Stock on 27 May 2004. *Brian Morrison*

Disputes with the Department for Transport

Most new franchises include a clause commonly known as 'Cap & Collar', which basically defines the revenue support and revenue sharing agreement between the Department for Transport and the franchise-holder. A target level of revenue is set and two threshold limits above and below the target are agreed for the franchise. Each of the thresholds signifies the extent of revenue support required, the 'Cap' being positive and the 'Collar' negative. If revenue falls beneath the negative thresholds, the DfT will provide revenue support; conversely, if it exceeds the positive thresholds the surplus is shared between the DfT and the franchisee.
In the case of the South West Trains franchise the agreement would only apply when the franchise reached its fourth year.

Stewart Palmer explained that South West Trains had a two-part dispute with the DfT concerning the interpretation of the 'Cap & Collar' clause in its franchise. The first was at what date revenue support should kick in. South West Trains believes it should be April 2010 via a 'look-back' condition, while the DfT believes it to be February 2011, arguing that there is no 'look-back' clause. Second, South West Trains firmly believes that whichever date is finally agreed upon, the income from its car park and certain other revenues should be excluded when determining whether the 'Cap & Collar' limits have been reached. This alone equates to around £15 million per year and the DfT argues that it should be included. During a recession-hit 2009 this is obviously a significant sum for the Train Operating Company.

Palmer added that South West Trains wanted to have the issues heard by the rail industry's own arbitration system, but the DfT did not agree, so ultimately the outcome will require a legal process and will most likely be settled in court. The former Managing Director emphasised that the dispute was not a request to renegotiate the franchise.

By midsummer 2009, highlighting the seriousness of the situation, Dan Milmo, transport correspondent for *The Guardian*, had reported through the business pages of the newspaper's website that the stand-off between some train operators and the government had 'erupted into open warfare'. Brian Souter is reported to have claimed that the Department for Transport might owe Stagecoach as much

BELOW: Class 458 'Juniper' set No 8021 enters Clapham Junction on 2 December 2008, forming the 17:09 South West Trains service from Reading to Waterloo. *Brian Morrison*

RIGHT: Seen under the impressive roof of Waterloo station is Class 444 set No 444016 together with three SWT inner-suburban Class 455 sets, the centre one being No 5866. *John Balmforth*

as £200 million, accusing the Department of being 'either dysfunctional or deceitful' over its failure to pay the company £1 million for consultancy work carried out by Stagecoach on the government's rail strategy. The South West Trains boss is reported to have said that the DfT had become 'chaotic' and its handling of the SWT franchise in particular was a 'dog's breakfast'. The Milmo article also reported that analysts were suggesting that the dispute showed the financial pressures being faced by the Department for Transport, which was already committed to investing around £3.4 billion a year in the UK's rail network. The DfT had hoped to offset a substantial portion of the receipts from franchise-holders against this, but had not foreseen the drop in passenger numbers the Train Operating Companies would encounter when it had signed off the franchises before the economic downturn.

In addition to the dispute over the inclusion of car park revenue under the 'Cap & Collar' clauses, Souter revealed further contractual disputes that, if successful, could cost the DfT in excess of £200 million:

- A £100 million dispute over when South West Trains qualifies for government support on revenue shortfalls
- Compensation for train operators in respect of forthcoming changes in ticket prices (2009), which Souter felt would cost South West Trains at least £20 million
- Adjustment of the financial terms of the SWT contract after the DfT delayed the introduction of new smartcard technology in stations. Souter said the impact could cost the company as much as £80 million.

Referring to the failure of the government to settle the £1 million Stagecoach bill for the consultancy work, Souter told Milmo, 'If they were a private company we would sue them,' accusing DfT officials of changing their minds over the smartcard issue as well as on other matters. He said that 'on some of these issues they have done 180-degree turns twice; you do have an issue about whether you can trust these people'. The disputes really reflected the huge pressure on the DfT amid a squeeze on public finances. Indeed, Douglas McNeill, an analyst at Astaire Securities, said: 'Mr Souter's comments suggest that the Department is at pains to conserve cash, due to the dawning realisation that it faces a huge bill for having underwritten optimistic passenger growth projections.'

Ultimately Stagecoach refused to submit to the DfT viewpoint as to the date the "Cap & Collar" arrangements should commence and by May 2010 gained a notable success in the dispute. It was reported in *Rail Professional* (issue 160, July 2010) that many analysts were predicting the victory would net the company an additional £100 million.

The positive side

On the positive side, passenger numbers had grown consistently with surprisingly little impact on commuter revenue in 2008 and early 2009. Car parking space at stations where South West Trains is the Station Facilities Owner is in huge demand by commuters and is nearly always full, having seen an increase in demand of around 50% over the last 10 years. During 2009 the TOC announced plans to provide an additional 2,000 parking spaces to manage the demand.

TOP: SWT Class 423 '4-VEP' set No 1319 is seen departing from Clapham Junction on the Down Main forming a Waterloo to Weymouth service. Another train made up of similar-vintage stock inherited with the franchise is seen heading in the opposite direction on its way to Waterloo. *South West Trains Picture Library*

BELOW: The 15:07 South West Trains service from Romsey to Salisbury makes the scheduled stop at Eastleigh on 22 May 2009, formed of Class 158 set No 158890 (ex-158815). *Brian Morrison*

LEFT: With Class 421/9 No 1304 resting in the yards outside Weymouth, Class 450 'Desiro' set No 450013 passes by on its way into the Dorset resort on 11 January 2004, with an SWT service from Waterloo. *Brian Morrison*

After Network Rail discontinued its comprehensive Great Britain National Rail timetable, South West Trains produced its own 288 page version. *Rail* magazine's feature writer Barry Doe, who is considered by many to be the UK's leading rail fares expert, described this as 'the best in the country'. In issue 636 of the magazine he pointed out that the publication includes all UK main-line operators' services with each table being allocated a table number, all of which are indicated on a system map. As well as an index of many stations, the timetable includes a number of tables for bus links within the SWT operating area.

South West Trains services call at 206 stations (232 prior to the December 2009 timetable change), including 185 where the company is the Station Facilities Owner. To recognise the hard work put in by its staff, the company holds its own 'South West Trains Station of the Year Awards', the competition being divided into four sections: best overall, best large, best medium and best small. The 2009 winners of the prestigious awards were:

- Best overall – Salisbury
- Best large – Guildford
- Best medium – Salisbury
- Best small – Staines.

Salisbury TCD – the UK's best-performing diesel rail depot

At the same time Salisbury Traincare Depot became the country's best-performing diesel depot. Some of the Class 158 and 159 diesel multiple-units (DMUs) serviced by the depot achieved an incredible 100,000 miles between breakdowns. In an interview with *Rail Professional* (November 2009), South West Trains' Engineering Director Christian Roth said, 'We don't really understand why other operators are so very far behind, but we have a very low staff turnover here and 70 per cent of the trains are stabled here each night, and all the engineering is done in-house not with outside suppliers or manufacturers.'

Located next to the city's station, Salisbury TCD dates from just before privatisation in 1993, having been established by the well-respected rail engineer Mac Macintosh, who served the company as Christian Roth's predecessor. It was, therefore, only right that he was invited to return to Salisbury to open a new £3 million train shed, built for the TOC in 2009 by BAM Nuttall, to provide facilities for trains to be refuelled and have their toilets emptied. At the ceremony Macintosh said, 'This is a people story. The 120 staff in Salisbury Traincare Depot are mainly ex-military, and many of the people

BELOW: SWT Class 159 set No 159004 awaits attention on No 6 road at Salisbury depot. The ground position light signal can be seen showing the two white lights at a 45-degree angle, giving the driver permission to enter the depot. *South West Trains Picture Library*

ABOVE: SWT Class 170/3 'Turbostar' set No 170306 receives attention at Salisbury Traincare Depot on 5 December 2006. *Brian Morrison*

LEFT: Class 159 set No 159018 is seen at Salisbury depot undergoing preparation for its next turn of duty. Note the 'Not To Be Moved' board attached to the train for staff safety purposes. *South West Trains Picture Library*

BELOW: Spotted in unfamiliar territory is South West Trains Class 158 set No 158883 as it passes through Peterborough on 10 July 2007 while on a works visit. *Rich Mackin/ railwayscene.co.uk*

ABOVE: SWT Class 159 set No 159012 passes Exmouth Junction as it works an Exeter St David's to Waterloo service. *South West Trains Picture Library*

RIGHT: The South West Trains 10:01 service from Paignton to Waterloo departs after the stop at Teignmouth on 24 May 2008, formed of Class 159/1 No 159104 and Class 159/0 No 159014. *Brian Morrison*

who joined 16 years ago are still here today.' He added, 'Money was even tighter then than it is now. We had a new depot and new trains, and it transformed the entire route. In the 1990s we had 24 trains, now we have 41, so the capacity of the shed has virtually doubled.' Most of the staff live locally, making SWT an important employer in the city. Their skills have halved the carriage preparation time to just 40 minutes, yet they still achieve an average of 30,000 miles per casualty. Fleet production manager John Parsons revealed his pride in this when he said, 'Nowhere else comes close. The nearest comparable DMU depot performance is ScotRail, and they only get 10,000 miles per casualty.'

The depot at Salisbury is located very close to people's homes, a street of terraced houses being separated from it by only a thin wire mesh fence, but because most of its work is carried out at night noise pollution is a significant factor. South West Trains admits that for a while it received many complaints about the noise, but the company explained that it does try to be a good neighbour and trains, having passed through the carriage cleaning wash, are now returned by gravity down the slope to the shed with their motors

turned off. At the opening ceremony for the new train shed, invited guests sampled the gravity transfer, which John Parsons described as 'a real conversation-stopper'. Head of the depot infrastructure, Clive Trencher, told *Rail Professional* that 'the main problem these days is vandalism and trespass, but it's just the usual kids' stuff because we're right in the middle of the city'.

CHAPTER SEVEN

The Lymington Branch

It could be argued that the Island Line services (described in the next chapter) are the quaintest operated by SWT, but without doubt the 5½-mile-long Lymington Branch is by far the most charming. Almost like the Isle of Wight rail services, the branch is virtually self-contained; its trains run only a short distance along the main Waterloo-Weymouth line from Brockenhurst station before diverging onto the single track Lymington Branch. En route trains pass through the New Forest National Park before calling briefly at Lymington Town station. They then continue across the picturesque harbour bridge before terminating at Lymington Pier station, setting down passengers just a few yards from the ferries.

In 1973 the then British Rail had introduced a car ferry service between Lymington and Yarmouth on the Isle of Wight, with considerable numbers of foot passengers arriving by train at Lymington Pier. When the safety certificates of the ferries expired in 2009 the ferry company replaced them with larger 'W Class' ships – an action which became the subject of legal activity in which it was alleged the larger vessels were causing harm to the mudflats and salt marshes of the river which are a haven for bird and marine life. In February 2009 the court issued a ruling agreeing with the objecting Lymington River Association but did not issue an order for the new ferry service to be suspended. Had it done so, it would almost certainly have seen the end of the Lymington Branch line as well as having a detrimental effect on the western end of the Isle of Wight.

Since privatisation of Britain's railways the line has been in the care of South West Trains and services have been operated by two ex-BR Class 421 4-CIG EMUs, which had to be shortened to three cars because of platform lengths. The platforms also required work and incredibly this was completed without the need to close the stations. Even so, this gave the company a substantial headache because the elderly 90mph EMUs were of the Mark 1 type. Even though the service required only one train to be operating at any one time and with a maximum line speed of 45mph, SWT felt they would be ideal for the job. Nevertheless, because of the national requirement to withdraw the much-loved (certainly by enthusiasts and many passengers) Mark 1 EMU slam-door rolling stock which operated along the branch from active service, it meant that the train operator had to make an application to HMRI for authority to keep them in service on the line. The company's then managing director, Andrew Haines, said: 'We believe this is the right way forward and rather than trying to justify the expensive costs of a new train, which would only be needed to cover a journey time of 10 minutes, it makes sense to refurbish two perfectly good slam-door trains.' In fact the timetable also only allowed a 5-minute turn-round and concern had been voiced by some that the alternative newer trains available did not have software that would be compatible with this.

The company was successful in its application and with the class nationally due to be taken out of revenue-earning service SWT grasped the opportunity to purchase two of the units outright. They remained under the umbrella of the operators Wimbledon TCD for maintenance purposes. During 2004 the newly purchased trains, originally built in 1971 by BREL at York, were refurbished and modified at Wimbledon to include the provision of wheelchair space and additional cycle storage, the trains being reclassified as Class 421/7 '3-CIG' units. At the same time they were fitted with headlights and a simple form of central door-locking, and repainted into heritage liveries: unit No 1498 received the 1950s BR green livery but with yellow front-end warning panel, and unit No 1497 the later 1970s BR blue/grey with full yellow front ends. The two units were named *Freshwater* and *Farringford* after two of the old Lymington-Yarmouth ferries. Despite being capable of 90mph, the dispensation meant that the two refurbished EMUs had to be specifically used on the Brockenhurst-Lymington Pier shuttle services.

When South West Trains announced its decision to purchase the two trains outright it said that doing so would help make the line more cost-effective thereby helping to safeguard its future, fitting perfectly with the Strategic Rail Authority's Community Rail Development Strategy, which involved looking at ways of making branch lines more cost-efficient. The Lymington line had already been proposed, and was subsequently successful in July 2008, as being suitable for a Community Rail Partnership (CRP). Chris Austin, the SRA's Executive Director for Community Rail Development, said: 'The aim of the Community Rail Strategy is to help safeguard the future of lines such as Lymington by putting them on a more sustainable footing and working with the local communities they serve to help increase passengers and make a greater contribution to local economic development. Lymington is a perfect example of this strategy at work and will help to give local people their say in the running, and invariably the future of their railway.'

The line has continued to be a success and by 2010 was carrying ever-increasing passenger numbers. Connections to ferries at Lymington Pier and main-line services at Brockenhurst have been successfully maintained despite its trains nearing their 40th anniversary, but age does eventually take its toll and they were due to be replaced on weekdays by Class 158 DMUs and 'Desiro' Class 450 sets at weekends by May 2010; the earlier rumours suggesting the use of 'Desiro' trainsets now proving to be correct. Many people will be sad to see them go but, as Stewart Palmer explained, the units had by now become very expensive to maintain and a good commercial case to keep them proved to be impossible to achieve. Despite this, SWT will continue working with Hampshire County and New Forest District councils to involve other stakeholders in the CRP. The only remaining threat to the line would appear to be the risk that the courts could prevent the new type of ferries from operating if it can be shown that they do cause damage to the river's ecology. Many local people certainly felt that the court victory was a hollow one, but with passenger numbers still increasing it cannot be denied that the rail service to the Isle of Wight via Lymington is popular.

CHAPTER EIGHT

Island Line: main-line rail services on the Isle of Wight

The Isle of Wight's main-line rail services followed their counterparts on the UK's mainland into privatisation when Stagecoach Holdings plc won rights to operate the island's rail services from 13 October 1996 for a term of five years. In a similar fashion to the early South West Trains franchise, that of Island Line was also extended without being put out to open tender in March 2001, when the Strategic Rail Authority authorised a two-year extension to the incumbent operator. Among the passenger benefits included in the extension were the right to a full refund of the fare paid (including ferry and mainland train service portions of the fare) if a service was delayed by 30 minutes or more, or two consecutive trains were cancelled. The Island Line franchise was further extended in December 2003 when the Strategic Rail Authority signed an agreement with Stagecoach Holdings plc for it to run on to February 2007, giving Island Line the same franchise end date as that of South West Trains.

Prior to 2007 Island Line had been the smallest of all the UK rail franchises, just 8½ miles in length, operating between Ryde Pier Head (connecting with ferry services to Portsmouth Harbour) and Shanklin. Despite this, it received two government Charter Marks for excellent service and has been designated a Community Rail Partnership. Island Line, which carried almost 1.5 million passengers in 2009, is used primarily by a mix of commuters travelling within the island, across to Portsmouth by ferry and, to a limited extent, onwards to London, as well as Isle of Wight residents making leisure journeys alongside holidaymakers and day tourists from the mainland.

When the Island Line franchise was re-let in 2007, the Department for Transport's policy of reducing the number of franchises had resulted

BELOW: Set No 006, of Island Line's former London Underground 1938 stock, makes its way along Ryde Pier en route from Shanklin to Ryde Pier Head in May 2009. *John Balmforth*

RIGHT: Resplendent in its recent red repaint, Island Line's Class 483 set No 006 passes the County Ground while forming a Ryde Pier Head to Shanklin service. *John Balmforth*

in franchise boundaries being redrawn. Part of this process required the previous South West Trains and Island Line franchises to be combined into a single franchise. Stagecoach created a new bidding vehicle, 'Stagecoach South Western Trains Ltd', through which it made the successful bid, subsequently taking the decision to continue operating the two railways under their existing public brandings despite their now being consolidated into a single Train Operating Company. A unique difference of the Isle of Wight franchise from those let on the mainland is the vertical integration between service operation, rolling stock and infrastructure, which makes the franchise-holder responsible for all. Many rail industry experts have voiced the opinion that this should be applicable throughout the UK's rail network, a viewpoint that has considerable merit, and the arrangement continued when the two franchises were merged.

The tiny Island Line Train Operating Company, like South West Trains, had previously been operated by Stagecoach, but as a legal entity in its own right with its own board of directors, while sharing the same chairman as South West Trains, thus ensuring a positive working relationship with its sister TOC across the Solent.

It has to be said that the main-line railway on the Isle of Wight has a special charm of its own, almost frozen in time as it provides services along its 8½-mile route. Operating in what seems to be a little world of its own, an absolute lifetime away from the railway most passengers know, it transports its users back in time to London's Underground system in pre-Second World War days; quite simply a transport delight which makes it worthwhile taking a brief glimpse at the Island's rail history.

The island once boasted some 53 miles of rail network containing 36 stations and halts. Even though the network became quite complex, history has shown that the remaining 8½ miles now operated by Island Line has always been thought of as the island's 'main line', but with the maximum running speed now restricted to 45mph. In 1948, when the island's rail services were amalgamated with the Southern Railway (one of the 'Big Four' companies formed as part of the 'grouping' of the British railway system in 1923), its new owner began to improve the well-used Isle of Wight's rail network, in particular the Ryde to Ventnor line. This included the provision of a passing loop at Wroxall and doubling of the track between Brading and Sandown. Further

BELOW: Four of Island Line's total fleet of six sets of Class 483 ex-London Underground 1938 stock can be seen at Ryde St John's Road in this photograph taken from the steps of the signalbox. The depot located next to the station can also be seen. *John Balmforth*

LEFT: Island Line's Class 483 set No 006 is seen again as it passes bridge No 18 at Truckells en route to Shanklin on 28 May 2009.
John Balmforth

plans to install double track through to Shanklin never materialised, but even so, the railway continued to prosper, boosted by the large numbers of summer passengers, and it easily competed with the arrival of the motor car. Nevertheless, at times there were attempts to remove the island's rail services completely, and the 1950s eventually witnessed the closure of much of the network. Despite this, the Ryde-Ventnor and Ryde-Newport-Cowes services continued to operate successfully right up to 1964, when Dr Beeching's controversial closure proposals for large areas of the UK's rail system were announced. His proposal to withdraw the remaining Isle of Wight routes received a great deal of opposition. It is now a matter of history that Dr Beeching's proposals for the Isle of Wight were defeated, and much celebrated on the island, but even so, islanders faced disappointment when the Newport-Cowes and Shanklin-Ventnor routes were still withdrawn, leaving only the Ryde-Shanklin section of main line that today's passengers know so well.

It should not be overlooked that railway preservationists have since reopened part of the island's closed rail routes, and the Isle of Wight Steam Railway today operates heritage services over part of the former Ryde-Newport line via Wootton, Havenstreet, Ashey and Smallbrook Junction, where passengers can connect with Island Line services.

When electrified by British Rail's Southern Region in the mid-1960s to remove steam traction from the island, it was found that normal railway rolling stock could not be used due to gauge clearances through the 391-yard-long tunnel at Ryde; headroom had been reduced following the withdrawal of steam-hauled services in order to improve track gradients. To overcome this, BR purchased a fleet of redundant London Underground tube stock dating from the 1920s and rebuilt it for use on the isolated network. This rolling stock became life-expired in the late 1980s and the then BR sub-sector Network SouthEast purchased some 'more modern' ex-tube stock dating from 1938, which had previously run on London Underground's Northern Line. Now TOPS-coded as Class 383, a number of these sets are still in service today, drawing power from the third rail 630V dc electricity supply. This in turn is fed from substations at Ryde, Rowborough and Sandown.

The line provides important transport links for islanders and tourists alike with the following stations:

- Ryde Pier Head, which opened on 12 July 1880, is located at the end of the pier; here passengers can connect with Wightlink's fast and frequent catamaran services to the mainland, where the ferry terminal is located adjacent to Portsmouth Harbour station. Some 127,514 passengers used the station during 2008/09.
- Ryde Esplanade opened on 5 April 1880, although it closed briefly to allow electrification work in 1967. It serves Ryde town centre and is, as its name suggests, located on the sea front where it forms part of the Ryde Transport Interchange. From here passengers can access the island's bus services as well as connecting hovercraft services to Southsea. For many it is the most convenient station for access to the town centre. The station saw 397,715 passengers

pass through in 2008/09 and its station buildings house the line's principal ticket office and lost property facilities.
- Ryde St John's Road opened on 23 August 1864 and is located 1½ miles south of Ryde Pier Head. In 2008/09 some 199,956 passengers used the station to access the residential area of the town, but it is also of strategic importance to Island Line because in addition to being the location of the line's signalbox, which has controlled Island Line's signalling since 1989, it also has a passing loop allowing two trains per hour to operate. The station is also the base for Island Line's administration team.
- Smallbrook Junction is one of the few UK main-line railway stations that have no outside public access. Opened on 20 July 1991 after the Isle of Wight Steam Railway was extended to reach the Island Line route, it provides a passenger interchange between the two railways, made use of by 4,458 passengers in 2008/09.
- Brading opened on 23 August 1864 and was originally built by the Isle of Wight Railway as an important junction station. Today Brading station is of less strategic importance to the island's rail network, but is still used by a healthy number of passengers – some 65,851 during 2008/09.
- Sandown, like its neighbour along the line at Brading, opened on 23 August 1864 as a junction station, seeing train services to Horringford, Merstone, Newport and Cowes, in addition to the stations it still serves today as part of Island Line. Its importance to residents, holidaymakers and tourists alike is highlighted by the 264,952 passengers using it in 2008/09.
- Lake station, opened on 11 May 1987, was the island's youngest until its cousin at Smallbrook Junction opened in 1991. It serves the village of Lake and its success is shown by the 67,316 Island Line passengers it saw in 2008/09.

TOP: Although a number of different signalling systems are in use on Island Line, old-style semaphore signals still survive. This example, seen at Ryde St John's Road on 28 May 2009, saw previous service on the mainland at Waterloo. *John Balmforth*

RIGHT: On the mainland old-style mechanical signalboxes are gradually being replaced by modern counterparts, but when the author visited in May 2009 this example on the Isle of Wight was still in everyday use at Ryde St John's Road. *John Balmforth*

- Shanklin, which is the modern-day terminus of the line, also opened its doors to rail passengers on 23 August 1864, at which time passengers could travel through to Ventnor. The station's second platform is no longer accessible by rail and today is home to a well-tended flowerbed, and its subway has long since been filled in. A small shop is available at the station, and it is the terminus of Rail Link buses to Ventnor and St Lawrence. In 2008/09 it was the line's second-busiest station, with 364,224 passing along its platform.

Island Line's Traincare Depot is located adjacent to Ryde St John's Road station and is home to the company's six two-car ex-London Underground electric multiple-units (EMUs), now designated Class 483. The depot has four roads, two of which have full repair facilities. Despite not being able to house the full fleet at the same time, the depot, which is the smallest to be found on the UK's main-line rail network, is well equipped and, while sometimes used as a train shed, is also capable of carrying out major overhauls as well as routine general maintenance. Four Matterson jacks have been provided to enable carriages to be lifted without using manual jacks, and a raised pitted road assists periodic inspection and maintenance of rolling stock. Carriage washing is done by hand.

Following the closure of signalboxes at Brading and Sandown, all of Island Line's train regulation is now controlled from the signalbox at Ryde St John's Road station:

- Ryde Pier Head to Ryde St John's Road – Track Circuit Block
- Ryde St John's Road to Sandown – Tokenless Block
- Sandown to Shanklin – One Train Working.

Maintenance of the signalling equipment is the responsibility of the franchise-holder, while renewals remain within Network Rail's remit.

The six remaining two-car trains rely heavily upon the skills of the depot engineers who tend their charges with loving care. Unfortunately the location has been prone to flooding, and both the depot and the adjoining Ryde St John's Road station have from time to time found themselves under water. Nevertheless, under the watchful eyes of depot manager Jeff Harper and his staff, the trains continue to receive high-quality maintenance and overhauls. The most serious issue the team faces tends to be that of rough riding and bogie component wear, which is partly due to the condition of the permanent way. The high-quality care provided at the depot is vital since, following its successful bid for the newly integrated franchise, the company admitted that it had no plans to replace the current Island Line rolling stock during the life of the franchise. Instead, a Stagecoach spokesperson explained that the company intends to invest to ensure the viability of the existing Island Line rolling stock and infrastructure. Leasing costs are an expensive item for any Train Operating Company, and in March 2009, South West Trains took the first steps to meet its promise by purchasing the stock outright (which by the end of the franchise will be almost 80 years old) from HSBC Rail.

When I interviewed Brian Souter during my research for this book he revealed his pride in Island Line, highlighting the unique vertical integration between the TOC and infrastructure maintenance, adding that he considers the company to have 'one of the best teams on the ground that you could come across on the railways'. Souter also emphasised that Island Line is consistently the best-performing railway in the UK. Stewart Palmer echoed this when he told me, 'Stagecoach hopes to keep Island Line running as a low-cost Community Railway, rationalise its track layout and move its passing loop to Brading in order to permit a 30-minute frequency.' This highly desirable aspiration would remove the confusion caused by the franchise's existing service pattern, which is skewed to 20/40-minute intervals in order to meet the Passenger Service Requirement, leaving a gap of 40 minutes between some services, although he did admit that the timescale for this is uncertain in the economic climate of 2009/10.

ABOVE: The newly repainted and refurbished Class 483 set No 008 waits outside the depot at Ryde St John's Road for final preparations before re-entering service on the Isle of Wight. *John Balmforth*

ABOVE: Island Line Class 483 set No 007 is seen alongside an unidentified sister unit undergoing maintenance inside Ryde St John's Road depot on 28 May 2009. *John Balmforth*

RIGHT: Class 483 bogie frames await the refitting of various component parts inside Ryde St John's Road depot while an engineer carries out remedial work to one of the train's door frames. *John Balmforth*

CHAPTER **NINE**

The South West Trains fleet, past and present

The South West Trains franchise has operated an interesting and varied fleet of trains, past and present, mainly consisting of third rail 750V dc electric multiple-units. The franchise inherited several old Mark 1 slam-door sets, which had mostly been replaced by 2005, an achievement of which Brian Souter told me he is extremely proud. The present-day South West Trains franchise uses some 340 trainsets (including the six used by Island Line to provide National Rail services on the Isle of Wight), with 299 drawing their power from the third rail 750/660V dc electricity supply. The remaining 41 trainsets are diesel-powered, with the addition of a solitary Class 73/2 electro-diesel locomotive. Despite consisting mainly of multiple-units (electric and diesel versions), with few locomotives, the fleet, both past and present, is much more varied than might at first be expected.

RIGHT: The cab controls of a Class 73 electro-diesel locomotive as used by South West Trains. *South West Trains Operations and Safety Training Centre*

BELOW: After privatisation SWT retained a fleet of three Class 73 dual-powered locomotives for depot transfer and 'Thunderbird' duties. The locomotives received full SWT livery and No 73109 carried nameplates *Battle of Britain 50th Anniversary*. *Rich Mackin/ railwayscene.co.uk*

Class 73 electro-diesel locomotives

Still in service with South West Trains at the time of research, and looked after by Bournemouth and Wimbledon Traincare Depots, the dual-powered 90mph (145kph) Class 73 electro-diesel locomotives are capable of operating by drawing power from the third rail 750V dc electricity power supply, or, where that is unavailable, by making use of their onboard diesel engines. South West Trains have operated three of the class, all of which received the full SWT outer-suburban blue livery; Nos 73201 and 73235 were on lease while the third, No 73109 *Battle of Britain*, was purchased outright. In South West Trains service they have been used mainly on depot transfer and 'Thunderbird' train rescue duties, although adapter couplers are required because the locomotives' couplers are not compatible with the rest of the fleet. By August 2009 only No 73235 remained in service with the company.

ABOVE: South West Trains' route-learning 'Bubble Car' unit No 96012 *John Cameron* (converted from Class 121 No 55028) is pictured at Salisbury on 11 May 2005. *Brian Morrison*

ABOVE RIGHT: The cab interior of South West Trains' solitary 'Bubble Car'. The unit was used mainly for driver route-learning purposes and is now preserved on the Swanage Railway. *J. A. Morgan/South West Trains*

RIGHT: Class 158 set No 158886 is seen making a station stop at Eastleigh on 24 May 2009. *Rich Mackin/ railwayscene.co.uk*

Class 121 (rebuilt as Class 960) 'Bubble Car'

A number of single-car DMUs, nicknamed 'Bubble Cars', were taken into departmental service when their passenger service days ended, where they continued to perform useful roles. Such a unit, Driving Motor Brake No 960012, which had carried fleet No 55028 during its service with British Rail, found itself in service with South West Trains where it was used mainly for driver route-learning purposes, providing up to 12 trainee drivers with a good view of the route. It was also equipped to carry out Sandite work if required.

Built by Pressed Steel in about 1960 to the BR Derby high-density design, these Class 121 units had a top speed of 70mph (113kph) with a driving cab at each end. This made them ideal for branch-line work, where many station termini did not have 'run-round' facilities, affording operators quick turn-round times. It was unusual for these units to carry nameplates, but No 960012 was chosen to carry the name *John Cameron* as well as receiving the full South West Trains outer-suburban blue livery. Mr Cameron, who had been a non-executive director of South West Trains, had occupied a similar role with British Rail in pre-privatisation days. He is also the owner of two preserved steam locomotives, 'A4' 'Pacific' No 60009 *Union of South Africa* and No 61994 *The Great Marquess*. The 'Bubble Car' was sold to the Swanage Railway in 2009, where it has been returned to original condition and repainted green.

Class 158 two-car DMUs

Built by British Rail Engineering Ltd (BREL) at Derby between 1989 and 1992, these versatile two-car 90mph (145kph) diesel multiple-units are used by a number of train operators across the UK on short-distance stopping local services

as well as long-distance cross-country services. The units are used mainly by South West Trains on services from Waterloo to Salisbury, Waterloo to Bristol Temple Meads and Salisbury to Romsey via Southampton Central. The company operates 11 of the class, which are leased from Porterbrook and allocated to Salisbury Traincare Depot for maintenance. All are painted in the company's white main-line livery, reflecting their regular use on long-distance services. In December 2009 some units were scheduled to replace the Class 421 '3-CIG' (Corridor Intermediate Guard) Mark 1 heritage slam-door stock on the Brockenhurst-Lymington Community Rail Line services, though at the time of writing this date had slipped to May 2010 – with talk of the replacements being 'Desiro' trains.

The carriages, 76ft 1¾in (23.21m) long, are constructed with aluminium body sides and bi-parting sliding plug-type doors giving saloon access at the carriage ends. The trains have a 2+2 seating layout in Standard Class (114 seats) and 2+1 in 1st Class (13 seats), and are fitted with toilet facilities. These versatile trains can run in multiple with sister units of Class 14x, 15x and 17x trains.

Class 159 three-car DMUs (SWT version)

Used on services between Waterloo and Salisbury, Bristol, Exeter St David's, Paignton, Plymouth and Penzance, the 30 units in use with South West Trains are leased from Porterbrook and have a top speed of 90mph (145kph). Built by BREL at Derby, the units were originally intended to be Class 158s, but were upgraded before entry into revenue-earning service. Like their Class 158 cousins, the units' carriages are 76ft 1¾in (23.21m) long with aluminium body sides in which bi-parting sliding plug-type doors give access to the saloon at the carriage ends. The Class 159 DMUs were introduced into service during 1992/93, fitted with a 2+2 seating layout in Standard Class (172 seats) and 2+1 in 1st Class (24 seats), together with toilet facilities. They can operate in multiple with sister units of Classes 14x, 15x and 17x. As befits the routes over which they operate, they are painted in the South West Trains white main-line livery and are looked after by the SWT dedicated diesel depot at Salisbury.

In April 2008, unit No 159007 gained a permanent place in railway lore when it was chosen to partake in bio-fuel trials. The fuel used in the trials, which ran for the remainder of the year, was a mixture of diesel, soya bean and rape seed oil. It was part of an experiment to find alternative fuels for the future, led by the Association of Train Operating Companies (ATOC). The trial required South West Trains DMU No 159007 to operate using the experimental fuel on the Exeter-Salisbury-London Waterloo route, with SWT engineers at Salisbury Traincare Depot monitoring its performance, including any effect on speed, engine wear and exhaust emissions. To ensure accurate results the experiment was conducted in all seasons.

Part of the way through the testing, as is well documented at 'therailwaycentre.com', SWT Senior Project Engineer Neil Ovenden said: 'The trial is going well and it has made no difference whatsoever to the performance of the train. We are pleased to be taking part in this exercise, as we were in one for low-sulphur diesel a couple of years ago, to help the industry look at the pros and cons of various fuel options.' Meanwhile ATOC's Director of Engineering, Ian Papworth, said: 'Bio-diesel is a relatively new fuel for the railways and one that needs to be carefully examined. ATOC is keen to explore and understand the potential of this fuel and discover its advantages and disadvantages on behalf of its members, so that they can make informed decisions on the fuel strategy.' He went on to explain that desk-top

ABOVE: The first time a South West Trains Class 158 operated west of Exeter St David's was on 30 September 2005, when set No 158789 formed the 07:10 Waterloo to Paignton service. The train is seen departing from the Dawlish station stop and heading towards Kennaway Tunnel. *Colin J. Marsden*

BELOW: Class 159 DMU set No 159020 traverses the Down Dawlish passing stormy seas while working the 14:20 Waterloo-Paignton service on 21 September 2006. *Colin J. Marsden*

TOP: South West Trains Class 159 set No 159102 is caught by the camera a long way from home as it passes through Doncaster on its return journey following a works visit. *South West Trains Picture Library*

ABOVE: The comfortable seating in the 1st Class compartment of SWT Class 159 set No 159019 is seen on 3 April 2009. *John Balmforth*

TOP RIGHT: With the sea wall under repair, Class 159 set No 159010 departs from Dawlish on 23 May 2008, forming the 12:20 South West Trains service from Waterloo to Plymouth. *Brian Morrison*

studies, static engine and now train trials to date show that railway locomotives and railcars can run successfully on the type of bio-fuel mix currently on the market.

The trial was a success in that it did not cause any damage to the train's engines or performance, but the cost of running using the experimental fuel was found to be more expensive than when using conventional diesel, so the ATOC/SWT trial was not progressed further. It is still possible that the rail industry will pursue the subject further but, apart from the important matter of cost, a considerable number of other issues still remain, including taxation and the fuel's overall sustainability.

Class 170 'Turbostar' DMUs

During the year 2000 South West Trains leased eight two-car Class 170/3 'Turbostar' DMUs from Porterbrook to support its existing Class 159 fleet. Built by Adtranz at Derby between 2000 and 2001, these 100mph (160kph) diesel-hydraulic multiple-units were ideally suited to work on the operator's longer-distance services. Painted in South West Trains' white main-line livery, they worked services between Waterloo and Salisbury, Reading and Brighton, and Southampton local services, occasionally venturing as far afield as Exeter St David's. Several TOCs still operate the Class 170s in the UK today, including First TransPennine Express, which took over the train's leases when South West Trains withdrew them at the end of 2006.

Class 410 '4-BEP', Class 411 '4-CEP' and Class 412 '4-BEP' EMUs

The Class 411 '4-CEP' (Corridor Electro Pneumatic brake) electric multiple-units were originally built for British Rail at Eastleigh Works between 1956 and 1963 for use on the newly electrified routes in Kent. The trains were formed of two outer driving motor cars, each fitted out with Standard Class seating in open saloons, and two intermediate trailer cars. One of the trailer vehicles was an open saloon containing Standard Class seating, while the second was of the corridor composite type containing both Standard and 1st Class seating. The majority of the class were of the '4-CEP' type, but a small number originally classified as '4-BEP' (Buffet Electro Pneumatic brake) units were built. These sets had one of the Standard Class trailer vehicles replaced by a buffet car and initially received the classification Class 410 '4-BEP'. British Rail recognised the need for the '4-CEP' fleet to be refurbished, and during the late 1970s and early 1980s the trains visited BR's Swindon Works where, as part of the upgrade, the guard's compartment was removed from both motor cars, the guard's accommodation being installed in an intermediate trailer. At the same time, as a result of a drop in demand from passengers, a number of the '4-BEP' sets had their buffet cars removed, leaving only seven of the type remaining in South West Trains service, which were immediately reclassified as Class 412 sets.

When Stagecoach won the initial South West Trains franchise, the company did not inherit any of the Class 411 '4-CEP' units, but it did receive the seven Class 412 '4-BEP' sets. However, a shortage of trainsets saw the company take a short-term lease on two Class 411 '4-CEP' EMUs. These were soon followed by more, and by 1998 some 29 sets were in service with the TOC. They were a regular sight on services to Portsmouth, Southampton, Bournemouth, Weymouth and the Lymington Pier branch. The '4-BEP' units had faster acceleration than their sister '4-CEP' trains, and by 2002 South West Trains had replaced their buffet trailers with Standard Class-only cars; the re-formed trains were not only faster but now had additional seating.

As part of South West Trains' franchise commitment to replace all slam-door rolling stock, the units were ultimately replaced by the new 'Desiro' Class 444 and 450 trains, many having given more than four decades of service to the railway. The '4-CEPs' and '4-BEPs' were withdrawn by SWT between December 2002 and September 2005.

Class 421 '3-CIG' and '4-CIG' EMUs

Built between 1964 and 1972 as replacement stock for use on the Brighton and Portsmouth main lines, the Class 421 '4-CIG' electric multiple-units would eventually earn the right to be looked upon as one of the most popular types of train in use across BR's busy Southern Region. It is also of interest that the use of an 'IG' suffix was the London, Brighton & South Coast Railway's telegraphic code for Brighton, on which route the units were first introduced. Built by BREL at York, the Class 421 differed from many multiple-units by having all four traction motors located on one non-driving motor coach (a carriage without a driving cab). The trains were delivered in two batches. Those built between 1964 and 1966 were known as 'Phase 1' units and were initially used on Brighton services, while the later batch, built between 1970 and 1972, were labelled 'Phase 2' units for use on services to Portsmouth. These slam-door EMUs were fitted with low-density seating, which passengers found to be extremely comfortable; also, unlike many modern-day trainsets and carriages, the seating in the '4-CIG' units lined up with the body-side windows, giving good external vision.

Stagecoach's winning franchise bid in 1996 meant that the newly formed Stagecoach South Western Trains Ltd inherited a fleet of 12 'Phase 2' units and 22 of the 'Phase 1' build; the latter had by now received modifications to give faster acceleration, earning them the nickname 'Greyhounds'. The fleet was further supplemented during 1997 when eight Class 421 '4-BIG' (Buffet Intermediate Guard) units were transferred from the Connex South Central fleet. Although the additional trains were fitted with a buffet counter, they were never used in South West Trains service, operating instead with the counters locked out of use. Within two years the '4-BIGs' found themselves stored out of use, although during 1999, South West Trains modified eight of the units into 'Greyhound' status, which saw them reclassified as Class 421/8 '4-CIG' sets. The modification included the removal of the buffet cars, which were replaced by trailers taken from Class 421 '4-CEP' (Corridor

TOP: In the early days of the SWT franchise old Mark 1 slam-door set No 1396 has just arrived at Southampton Central, forming a Waterloo to Bournemouth service. *Andy Healey*

MIDDLE: The final official slam-door service from Waterloo is seen on 25 May 2005. The 11:35 service to Bournemouth consisted of Class 421/8 'Greyhounds' Nos 1396 and 1399 with Class 423 '4-VEP' No 3536 in the centre. *Brian Morrison*

ABOVE: Passing Lymington Junction, Brockenhurst, on 9 July 2005, Class 421 '3-CIG' No 1498 *Farringford* forms the branch service to Lymington Pier. *Brian Morrison*

ABOVE: South West Trains heritage Mark 1 slam-door Class 421 '3-CIG' set No 1497 *Freshwater*, painted in British Rail blue and grey, is seen on display at Eastleigh Works Open Day on 24 May 2009. *Rich Mackin/ railwayscene.co.uk*

RIGHT: The driver's controls of a Class 421 '4-CIG' EMU. *Colin J. Marsden*

BELOW: After its naming ceremony, blue-liveried Class 423 '4-VEP' No 3417 *Gordon Pettit* awaits departure from Waterloo on 2 June 2004, complete with route code 91. *Brian Morrison*

Electro Pneumatic brake) units when those sets were reduced to three-car units. The converted trailers quickly became popular with passengers, who appreciated their InterCity 1970s-style seating.

By mid-2004 a programme of withdrawing the Class 421s from revenue-earning service had commenced, the units being replaced by the new Siemens-built 'Desiro' trainsets. The final Class 421 '4-CIG' train to operate in South West Trains service – made up of units Nos 1396 and 1398 coupled to their cousin '4-VEP' (Vestibuled Electro Pneumatic brake) No 3536 – ran on 26 May 2005, forming a service from London Waterloo to Bournemouth.

Class 423 '4-VEP' EMUs

The four-car Class 423 '4-VEP' EMUs, built for British Rail between 1967 and 1974 by BREL at York, were used extensively on all three divisions of the Southern Region. In total 194 units were built, able to run at a maximum speed of 90mph and powered by a central power car. The sets contained 1st Class compartment seating and a mixture of high-density 2+2 and 2+3 seating in Standard Class. They soon found favour with passengers by virtue of their comfortable seating and individual access doors to each seating bay, which made the trains ideal for commuter services. In the late 1970s some of the units were converted for use on the Victoria-Gatwick Airport route, but just before privatisation the remaining sets underwent a partial refurbishment in which around half of the large luggage van area was fitted with Standard Class seating and the trains were reclassified as Class 423/4. Following privatisation the trains were split between the South West Trains and the ill-fated Connex franchises, and by 1999 a batch of 19 units underwent a more radical refurbishment in which all 1st Class accommodation was removed and replaced with open side-access Standard Class seating. At the same time the units were again reclassified, this time as Class 423 '4-VOP' (Vestibuled Open Plan).

The trains gave good service to South West Trains until they were withdrawn in May 2005 as part of the programme to remove all slam-door stock from the TOC's fleet. One unit, No 3417, was retained for railtour work, but was eventually sold to the Bluebell Railway for preservation.

Class 442 '5-WES' EMUs

During the 1980s British Rail found itself needing to replace the ageing rolling stock in use on the Waterloo-Bournemouth-Weymouth route. At the same time it also received authorisation to electrify the route between Bournemouth and Weymouth, which had an important bearing on the choice of the replacement trains. Ultimately a fleet of 24 high-specification five-car electric multiple-units based upon the Mark 3 rolling stock design was ordered from BREL, Derby. Delivered to British Rail in 1988/89, they were considered by some to be the 'Rolls-Royce' of EMUs, incorporating swing plug passenger doors and the use of a central power car.

Now leased from Angel Trains, these five-car EMU sets, alpha-coded '5-WES' (Wessex Electric Stock), or 'Wessex Electrics' as they became fondly known, built in 1988/89, were inherited by South West Trains at the

TOP LEFT: The 14:00 SWT service from Weymouth to Waterloo departs from Wareham on 12 April 2006, formed of Class 442 'Wessex Electric' No 2409 *Bournemouth Orchestras. Brian Morrison*

TOP RIGHT: The last scheduled Class 442 working from Waterloo resulted in photographers and enthusiasts being out in force. 'Wessex Electrics' Nos 2407 *Thomas Hardy* and 2417 *Woking Homes* await departure as the 18:35 SWT service to Bournemouth and Weymouth on 13 January 2007. *Brian Morrison*

MIDDLE: One of South West Trains' Class 442 'Wessex Electric' trains departs from Bournemouth in 2003 with a service for Waterloo, while in the background a Class 47 locomotive is carrying out a shunting manoeuvre. *South West Trains Picture Library*

BELOW LEFT:
Despite their age the Class 442 'Wessex Electric' sets still have the look of a modern train, the SWT white main-line livery suiting them very well. *Rich Mackin/ railwayscene.co.uk*

BELOW RIGHT: The Standard Class interior of the popular (with passengers) '5-WES' Class 442 'Wessex Electrics', showing the spacious accommodation and 2+2 seating layout. *Rich Mackin/ railwayscene.co.uk*

beginning of its franchise. Allocated to Bournemouth Traincare Depot, they provided a high-specification train capable of 100mph (160kph), drawing their power from the 750V dc third rail electricity supply. Painted in the company's white main-line livery and featuring 50 1st Class seats and 290 Standard Class seats in a 2+2 arrangement, the trains quickly became popular with passengers, some sets being used on Waterloo-Portsmouth Harbour services in addition to those serving Weymouth. Despite their popularity, the '5 WES' sets were not without their problems, and early in the South West Trains initial franchise they developed a series of hot axle boxes caused by grease contamination, which culminated in the sets being temporarily withdrawn from service. The resulting service cancellations saw the company handed a £1 million fine, which, even today, Brian Souter considers to have been very harsh. Many rail industry commentators, including myself, agree with him.

Stewart Palmer accepted that the trains were very popular with passengers, but pointed out that their electrical equipment was around 30 years old and not very reliable. He felt that it was only the exceptional dedication and expertise of the engineers at Bournemouth TCD that kept them going. The replacement of the sets was a key component of the successful 2007 franchise bid (and also featured in some of the losing bids), which required South West Trains to provide more capacity, and this resulted in them being replaced by Class 458 'Juniper' sets.

In February 2007, following the successful retention of the South West Trains franchise by Stagecoach, a combination of the mass withdrawal of slam-door rolling stock and the successful introduction of the Class 444 and 450 'Desiro' trainsets enabled South West Trains to achieve its franchise commitment, and the Class 442s were returned to the owning ROSCO, Angel Trains, which placed them in storage. Some of the sets have subsequently found further work with Southern/Gatwick Express.

Class 444 five-car and Class 450 four-car 'Desiro' EMUs

South West Trains had announced its intention to replace the ageing fleet of Mark 1 slam-door rolling stock by the end of 2004 because the trains had become increasingly unreliable and difficult to maintain, so it is worth taking an in-depth look behind the scenes at the introduction of the 'Desiro' trainsets that replaced them.

As part of the replacement programme, agreement was reached whereby Angel Trains, the Rolling Stock Operating Company (ROSCO), would purchase 172 new Siemens 'Desiro' Class 444 and 450 100mph (160kph) trainsets, which would then be leased to South West Trains. Understandably, a Train Operating Company rarely risks purchasing rolling stock outright (the exception in South West Trains' case being the aforementioned purchase of the one Class 73/1 electro-diesel locomotive and the pair of heritage Class 421 '3-CIG' slam-door Mark 1 EMUs, which it painted in heritage liveries for use on the Brockenhurst-Lymington branch). To do so would be commercially unsound, because any operator with a comparatively short franchise

RIGHT: South West Trains 'Desiro' Class 444 set No 444022 is seen arriving at Basingstoke's Platform 1 with a Waterloo to Poole service on 3 July 2009. *John Balmforth*

TOP LEFT: Class 444 set No 444016 is seen passing Upwey heading for Weymouth with a service from Waterloo. *South West Trains Picture Library*

ABOVE: The driver's cab controls of Class 444 and 450 'Desiro' EMUs. *John Balmforth*

LEFT: South West Trains 'Desiro' Class 444 set No 444012 passes Northam depot, Southampton, at speed in April 2009. *John Balmforth*

would not have time to achieve a suitable return on its investment. Instead, trains are leased from one of the ROSCOs, with the leasing charges being calculated over the anticipated lifetime of the trains, a much longer period of time than any of the UK rail franchises themselves. The 'Desiro' Class 444 and 450 fleets are a good example of this, since the cost of the new trains is in the region of £1.25 million per vehicle (Class 444) and £750,000 per vehicle (Class 450).

The order for the new 'Desiro' trainsets, which cover in excess of 21 million miles every year, was the biggest for new rolling stock by a UK train operator since privatisation. Originally both the Class 444 and Class 450 fleets were ordered as five-car sets; however, the Class 450 order was cancelled before the trains were built and replaced with a new order for four-car sets, the original order instead becoming part of the Class 350 sets used by other operators. The design of both classes to be used by South West Trains included:

- modular design
- air-conditioning
- audio/visual passenger information systems
- train management systems
- CCTV
- electronic sliding doors.

The total provision contract included full maintenance support and availability, together with reliability guarantees.

Recognising that the highly technical nature of the trainsets, which were built between 2002 and 2007, required specialised maintenance facilities, construction of a new Traincare Depot at Northam, Southampton, commenced in October 2001 in readiness for the arrival of the new trains (see Chapter 5). Once complete, South West Trains and Siemens turned their

RIGHT: Pictured in July 2009 at Basingstoke's Platforms 4 and 1 are SWT 'Desiro' Class 444 set No 444004 and Class 450 set No 450105. *John Balmforth*

BELOW: The driving car from 'Desiro' set No 444034 suffers the indignity of being caught on camera during transfer by road as it passes through Westbourne with a police escort en route to Crewe. *Paul S. Edwards*

BOTTOM: 'Desiro' set No 450101 is seen undergoing repairs after returning to the works at Düsseldorf, Germany. It had sustained damage during a derailment while under test in Belgium. *Paul S. Edwards*

attention to the testing of the new trains and training the staff that would be looking after them. All trains that operate on the UK's main-line rail network are required to have a safety case, and even though they were brand-new, the 'Desiros' were no different. Without a safety case they cannot run on the tracks when other services are operating. As a consequence the new 'Desiros' generally underwent testing overnight, and this usually took place near the Weymouth end of the line. In addition, South West Trains and Siemens needed to provide staff with high-quality training in the trains' use. Faced with the difficulty of providing this while the trains were still undergoing overnight testing, the two companies arranged for one of the sets to be taken by road to a training facility at Shoeburyness, where the staff were able to gain 'hands-on' experience in addition to classroom tuition.

The trainsets themselves underwent thorough testing at two locations. The first of these was at Siemens' purpose-built test centre near Wildenrath, Germany. The centre has a 28-kilometre track as well as an ultra-modern engineering section. This ensured that just about any kind of test required, and with any variation, could be carried out. To assist with this the entire South West Trains route infrastructure over which the trainsets would run was recorded by a test train and the data used by Siemens to put the 'Desiro' through its paces. Interestingly, because of a variation in voltage the German Government had to provide a special dispensation for the testing to be conducted; this was because of the need to

TOP: Several partially completed Class 450 sets due for eventual service with South West Trains stand in the open air at Wildenrath, Germany, in January 2000. *Paul S. Edwards*

LEFT: More 'Desiro' Class 450 sets for South West Trains are seen in the storage yards at Wildenrath awaiting completion in January 2000. *Paul S. Edwards*

BELOW: The future South West Trains sets Nos 444005 and 444031 await commissioning at Bournemouth TCD. *Paul S. Edwards*

leave the third rail power supply exposed – Germany has none. South West Trains could not 'sign off' the 'Desiro' until it had completed 1,000 kilometres at this stage of testing. When this milestone was reached, the South West Trains VIP party, visiting to inspect the trains, witnessed the previously recorded data for Clapham Junction being used for the test.

The second location selected was on Network Rail's main lines near Weymouth. After each night of test running had been completed, the trainsets had to be left in a safe state so that they were not a risk to other rail users. This saw them stored in a 'wheels-free zone' with their connector shoes isolated and wheels locked. In January 2003 the first 'Desiro' entered the brand-new Northam TCD, being dragged under test conditions from the 'wheels-free zone' for checking over. Eddie Milligan pointed out that the 'DESIRO = Desired One' design was easily interchangeable with third rail 750V dc or 25kW ac overhead power supply lines.

The 'Desiros' are unique in that their bodies are built entirely from aluminium – approximately 40% of each vehicle. They also have 'anti-climbing' teeth fitted to the vehicle

ends to greatly reduce the risk of carriages climbing onto each other in the event of a collision. All Class 444 bodies were built and assembled at the Siemens factory in Vienna, Austria, with the bogies etc being constructed not far away at Graz. The driving cars of the Class 450s were also built in Vienna, with their two centre trailers being built at the Uerdingen plant in Krefeld, Germany. Both classes are able to run on the UK's existing infrastructure, but, as Eddie Milligan explained, the network's power loading had to be 'beefed up'. Rheostatic and friction brakes are fitted and the trains are

RIGHT: On a wet December day in 2007 a Class 455/5 set and Class 450 set No 450004 stand at Waterloo alongside the former Eurostar London terminus. The Class 455/5 is preparing to form the regular Waterloo to Waterloo via Richmond service on route 32. *Rich Mackin/ railwayscene.co.uk*

BELOW: A goodly number of customers await SWT 'Desiro' Class 450 set No 450026 as it arrives under the newly restored roof at Bournemouth station. *South West Trains Picture Library*

capable of recycling unused power back into network via the third rail. The trains protect themselves in the event of power surges at 900V or higher, but conversely most modern train electronics do not like low voltages either, so there is further built-in protection to prevent it dropping below 480V. If voltage does drop too low, the protection system will shut down the trainsets. The built-in system also looks for high voltage surges, such as occur during lightning strikes, or when notching off. The instant interruption of current causes a spike of 50Hz, which is the same frequency as that used by the signalling system, so the trains have built-in 50Hz monitors that look for spikes irrespective of cause. The monitor measures the dc link voltage and if it detects a problem it opens the contactors of the trainsets' Auxiliary Control Unit and the High Speed Circuit Breaker, thus protecting the signals. These will then reset automatically if the fault is spurious, but if it is continuous they will 'lock out', affording protection. Eddie Milligan explained that the potential clash with signalling systems existed for around three years, but eventually it was proved that the source of the problem did not lie with the 'Desiro'. He felt that safety cases were overly cautious.

The 45-strong Class 444 fleet consists of five-car sets, each fitted with low-density 2+2 seating throughout, the exception being a 2+1 arrangement in 1st Class. Access is gained via a single passenger-operated plug leaf door at each end of the coach. Each vehicle has through gangway connections to adjoining vehicles and the sets can operate in multiple. They were principally intended for use on the long-distance Waterloo to Weymouth and Portsmouth Harbour services and therefore received the South West Trains white main-line livery; they have proved to be extremely popular with passengers.

Numerically larger, the 127-strong Class 450 versions each consist of four cars in which seating is 2+2 in 1st Class, and a combination of 2+2 and 2+3 in Standard Class. Access to carriages is via bi-parting sliding doors at one-third and two-thirds distance along the vehicle. As with their Class 444 cousins, through gangways are provided giving access between neighbouring vehicles, and the sets can, and frequently do, operate in multiple. The trains are painted in the blue livery adopted by South West Trains for its outer-suburban services. Responding to the need for extra capacity, particularly on the routes to Windsor, 28 of the sets were modified in 2008 and classified as Class 450/1 High Capacity sets, with the removal of 1st Class accommodation and the installation of 2+3 seating throughout. These units, which are easily identifiable by the letters 'HC' above the fleet number on the front of the trainsets, are usually found, though not exclusively, hard at work on the TOC's outer-suburban routes between Waterloo and Portsmouth Harbour, between Waterloo and Southampton Central and Bournemouth, and on the Windsor and Hounslow loop lines.

The 'Desiro' Class 444 and 450 fleets will be due for major overhaul from around May 2010, and Siemens has leased space at the reopened Eastleigh Works in Hampshire, just a short distance from the sets' Northam TCD home base, where it will carry out most of the work itself, the exception being work on the bogies, which will be done by Unipart Rail at Doncaster. The work will be split into four sections:

- power bogies
- trailer bogies
- air supply and brakes
- electrical.

Interestingly, the Class 444s will be the first 'Southern Region' trains to visit the Hampshire site since the Class 455 refurbishment was completed in 2005, just before the original closure of the works.

Class 450 ergonomics assessment

Shortly after the Class 450 sets were introduced on Waterloo-Portsmouth services, South West Trains received criticism from some passengers who suggested the seating layout was uncomfortable, presenting possible risks to passengers' health including, but not limited to, back pain and deep vein thrombosis (DVT). Concerned at this potential threat to its customers' health, the TOC commissioned a specialist company, Interfleet Technology Ltd, to undertake an independent assessment of the seating design and layout and to benchmark it against that of comparable classes, together with a review of existing evidence and research relating to the link between seating design and health.

The review used existing appropriate anthropometric data based on an estimated male/female ratio of 90:10, which is believed to be more representative of the commuter population than the traditional 50:50 ratio. With increasing passenger numbers there has been a trend towards a higher seating capacity on regional routes in Standard Class accommodation to reduce the numbers of passengers having to stand. The requirement to maintain suitable aisle width, coupled with other space restraints within vehicles, makes 3+2 seating a compromise rather than ideal. The review indicated that the risk of travel-related DVT was negligible without the existence of predisposing risk factors in an

LEFT: SWT 'Desiro' Class 450 set No 450012 arrives at Basingstoke's Platform 1 on 3 July 2009, while in the background another SWT 'Desiro' Class 444 set, No 444004, passes heading for Waterloo. *John Balmforth*

TOP: A view showing the pleasant interior of a 1st Class carriage of a South West Trains 'Desiro' Class 444 set. *South West Trains Picture Library*

MIDDLE: The Standard Class interior of an SWT 'Desiro' Class 450 High Capacity set. Note the 2+3 seating layout. *John Balmforth*

RIGHT: The Standard Class interior of a South West Trains 'Desiro' Class 444 set. The 2+2 seating layout is much appreciated by passengers travelling long distances. *South West Trains Picture Library*

individual. Furthermore, no studies identified the occurrence of DVT on journeys of the length of those taken on the Waterloo-Portsmouth route.

A summary of the review's findings, published by South West Trains on its website, states:

> *'...because there is some evidence that Whole Body Vibration (WBV) may be a contributory factor in the development of back pain, this issue was included in the review. The level of WBV experienced is the result of seating design, vehicle design and track quality. There are no UK rail industry standards for acceptable levels of exposure, but guidance issued by the Rail Safety and Standards Board in response to European Union Directive 2002/44/EC suggests that the level of experience to staff working on the trains is unlikely to reach levels requiring action. Given that the level of exposure to passengers is very unlikely to be greater than that of employees who work on trains, the likelihood of WBV causing medical harm to passengers is considered to be minimal.'*

The summary reveals that, as with all of the vehicles surveyed, there are some elements of the Class 450 design that limit the percentage of the population that can be physically accommodated, but the review did look at current best practice for provision of seating for a number of different applications, not just trains. The report concluded:

> *'The independent assessment confirms that there is nothing ergonomically wrong with the Class 450 seating and that it meets current best practice for the provision of seating, in many areas at the better end of the scale.*
>
> *When comparing seat width to hip breadth, the assessment identified that approximately 84% of the population would be accommodated by the Class 450 seat pan design. However, it does recognise that there are some issues with seat width, and based on the available anthropometric data that, when all seats are occupied, based on the 90:10 population,*

59% of the population will exceed their seating envelope with their elbows. This, however; is a comfort issue and not a health risk.

As part of the assessment exercise, 19 other Train Operators were contacted and asked if they had any seating health issues reported. No instances of DVT or back pain were found to have been reported by Train Operators operating 3+2 seating on comparable routes to South West Trains.

It is therefore reasonable to conclude that the criticism received is due more to comparison between the Class 444 and Class 450 than the actual design of the Class 450 seating.'

Class 455 four-car EMUs

Extremely well known to passengers using South West Trains' London inner-suburban services, the fleet of 91 Class 455/7, 455/8 and 455/9 four-car electric multiple-units in service with South West Trains were originally introduced under British Rail's stewardship in 1984/85. The earlier batch, which now forms the Class 455/8 series, is easily distinguishable by the 'rugged front-end design' of their cabs, when compared to the more stylish smooth-rounded cab roofs of their younger sisters. All three sub-classes were built by BREL at York, although the Class 455/7 sets were originally configured in three-car formation. Due to the need for increased capacity, those sets were increased to four cars by the addition of a Trailer Standard Open (TSO) vehicle taken from the Class 508 sets transferred to the Liverpool area by BR in 1984. The re-formed units are still to be seen giving sterling service today with both South West Trains and Southern.

When the UK's railways were privatised all the Class 455 EMUs passed into the ownership of two of the newly formed Rolling Stock Operating Companies, HSBC and Porterbrook; all of those under lease to South West Trains were from Porterbrook. Between 2003 and 2008, all 91 Class 455 sets in the SWT fleet underwent a radical refurbishment costing some £65 million, carried out by Bombardier at its Chart Leacon depot. They returned to service

ABOVE: Nowadays it is not unusual to find trains carrying an all-over livery for special occasions, or even simply plain advertising. SWT Class 455 set No 5868 is seen at Waterloo on 6 September 2005 in a special livery celebrating the Golden Jubilee of HM Queen Elizabeth II. *Rich Mackin/ railwayscene.co.uk*

LEFT: Inner Suburban set No 5750 en route to Waterloo, having just left Clapham Junction. *John Balmforth*

BELOW: Standard Class seating in the SWT Class 455/7 and Class 455/9 sets is of 2+2 arrangement, increasing to 2+3 in Class 455/8 sets. All of the South West Trains carriages contain electronic passenger information displays. *John Balmforth*

having been repainted in the bright red inner-suburban livery used by South West Trains, and such was the high quality of the refurbishment that some industry commentators reported that passengers were convinced that the trains were brand-new.

These EMUs, which have a maximum speed of 75mph (120kph), draw their operating power from the third rail 750V dc electric power supply. They are Standard Class only, and are fitted with 244 seats in a 2+2 arrangement, the exception being the Class 455/8 sets, which have a 2+3 high-capacity arrangement. Bodywork is of steel construction with the exception of the TSO vehicles found in the Class 455/7 units, which are of aluminium. External doors are of the bi-parting sliding type located at one-third and two-thirds locations. The trains have gangway connections throughout, and can operate in multiple with sister Class 455 units as well as Class 456 sets. All three Class 455 sub-classes are maintained at the South West Trains Wimbledon Traincare Depot.

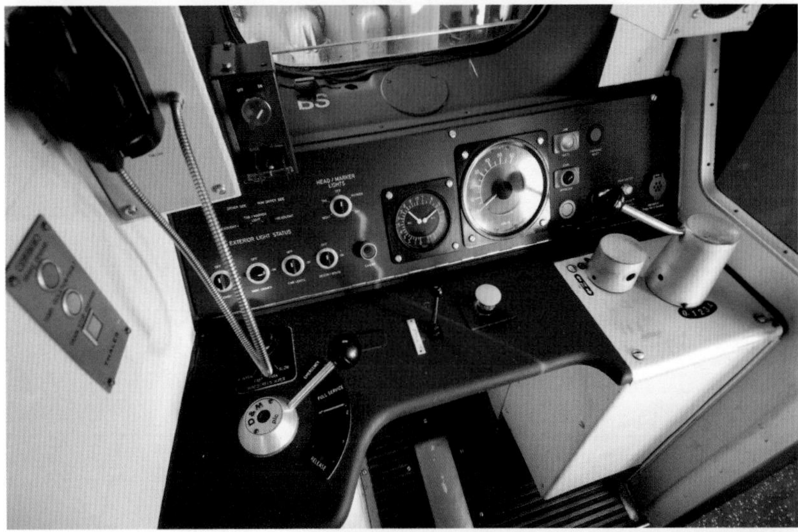

ABOVE: The driver's cab controls of a South West Trains Class 455 inner suburban set. *South West Trains Picture Library*

Class 458 '4-JOP' four-car EMUs

South West Trains operates 30 of these trainsets, which were first introduced between 1999 and 2002 for use on its outer-suburban services. Built by Alstom at its Washwood Heath, Birmingham, factory, the sets formed the Class 458 'Juniper' electric multiple-units, receiving the alpha-code '4-JOP'. This signified that the units consisted of four cars and were 'Juniper' Outer-suburban units owned by Porterbrook, although they were sometimes referred to as 'Juniper' Open Plan.

Seating is of the High Capacity design, providing 274 seats; this makes the trains ideally suited to the workload they carry out in South West Trains service. Bi-parting sliding plug doors located at one-third and two-thirds positions ensure that passengers can board and disembark quickly. The need for the trains to be able to operate in multiple resulted in them being built with front-end doors, permitting gangways throughout the trains when running in multiple with other units. However, this has led, perhaps unfairly, to many describing the trains as some of the ugliest ever built.

Although a comparatively modern design, the sets soon found themselves out of favour, with operators preferring the newer Siemens-built 'Desiro' trains, and the decision was taken to withdraw the Class 458s from service by the end

RIGHT: SWT Class 458 sets Nos 8008 and 8022 are seen between turns, keeping company with a Class 421 heritage train of Mark 1 stock and a 'Wessex Electric' Class 442 set at Bournemouth TCD. *South West Trains Picture Library*

of 2006. Worse was to follow when, in mid-2006, the trainsets fell foul of the UK's new Disability Discrimination Act. The new regulations dictated that the sets be taken out of use because their electronic passenger information system displays were 'too small'. Many people regarded the loss of otherwise perfectly good trainsets from service as the result of 'barmy red tape', though all was not lost when, following the successful bid by Stagecoach to retain the franchise in 2007, all 30 of the sets were brought up to the latest operational standards and put back into revenue-earning service by South West Trains. They were allocated to Wimbledon Traincare Depot for maintenance, under whose care they remain today.

Despite being used on the outer-suburban network, mainly the Waterloo to Reading, Ascot and Guildford routes, the trains carry the South West Trains main-line white livery, though strictly speaking they should carry the blue livery as worn by the Class 450 'Desiro' trainsets. Managing Director Stewart Palmer told me that he would like to get them repainted into their correct livery, but in the 2009 economic recession to do so would just not make commercial sense.

Class 483 two-car EMUs

By 2007, when the news broke that Stagecoach had been selected to operate the new South West Trains franchise, its predecessor and that of Island Line had been merged into a single franchise. Although Island Line has its own dedicated chapter in this book, it seems sensible to include its rolling stock with the rest of the fleet in this chapter covering the South West Trains fleet.

ABOVE LEFT: The driver's controls of an SWT Class 458 'Juniper' EMU set used on outer-suburban services. *South West Trains*

ABOVE RIGHT: The bright red upholstery of the 2+3 high-capacity seating in the Standard Class coaches of SWT Class 458 'Juniper' sets provides a pleasant ambience for the trains' interior. *John Balmforth*

BELOW: One of Island Line's Class 483 sets arrives at Brading in May 2009 while working a Shanklin to Ryde Pier Head service. Despite being more than 70 years old, these trains still give sterling service. *John Balmforth*

ABOVE: The interior of newly refurbished Island Line Class 483 set No 008. The refurbishment has clearly been carried out to a very high standard. *John Balmforth*

Due to gauge clearance restrictions in the tunnel at Ryde, British Rail had, in the mid-1960s, purchased a number of ex-London Underground tube stock sets of 1920s vintage to replace the withdrawn steam-hauled services. However, by the mid-1980s the stock had become life-expired and BR again turned to London Underground to purchase some more 'modern' ex-tube stock, this time dating from 1938. Island Line later rebuilt the trains into twin power-car sets, which now operate in either two- or four-car formations, drawing power from a third rail 630V dc supply.

The sets are allocated to Ryde St John's Road depot for general maintenance and overhaul, with support from London Underground's Acton Works, which is a source of spares and also reconditions key components. The trains have London Underground-style group and longitudinal seating with crew-operated sliding doors. Designated Class 483, they have appeared in a variety of liveries, some being painted blue with dinosaur pictures, others in mock London Transport red or 'heritage liveries'.

Today just six two-car sets remain in service, all having been given London Underground red paintwork (but without London Transport roundels), and with a small yellow warning panel at the cab ends.

The South West Trains fleet in the preservation world

The South West Trains fleet, both past and present, has consisted mainly of EMUs and DMUs. They all have fast acceleration and the ability to transport large numbers of passengers, whether commuters or leisure travellers. Even so, many people perceive them to be somewhat boring simply because they are not locomotive-hauled (although the goodly numbers of trainspotters seen at many stations around the South West Trains network tend to suggest that this may be something of a myth), conveniently overlooking the fact that they have given long service as well as being environmentally friendly, a fact supported by the clamour for more rail electrification schemes in the modern world.

Whether boring or not, the trains have been successful and a number of units or carriages retired from South West Trains have found their way into the world of preserved railways, where they continue to give loyal service. Some examples known to the author are listed here, although the list is by no means exhaustive:

Locomotive/unit class	Vehicle number	Present location
Class 73		
Electro-diesel locomotive	73109 *Battle of Britain*	Swanage Railway
Class 411 EMU		
1198 '3-CEP'	70508	Dartmoor Railway
Class 412 EMU		
2311 '4-BEP'	61804/70607/70539/61805	Eden Valley Railway
2315 '4-BEP'	61798/70354/70229/61799	Eden Valley Railway
2325 '4-BEP'	61229/70235/69345/61230	East Kent Railway
Class 421 EMU		
1392 '4-CIG/CEP'	70273	Dean Forest Railway
1499 '3-CIG'		Dean Forest Railway
1393 '4-CIG/CEP'	70527	Great Central Railway
1399 '4-CIG/CEP'	70508	Dartmoor Railway
Class 423 EMU		
3417 '4-VEP'		Bluebell Railway

CHAPTER TEN

South West Trains: the future

Company boss Brian Souter told me in a refreshingly honest in-depth interview that he keeps a close eye on all matters Stagecoach, but believes in allowing his individual companies to be run with little interference, thus encouraging innovation on the part of its managers. Souter also reminded me of his confidence in, and gratitude for, the workforce, giving them the credit for South West Trains continually being near the top of the Customer Satisfaction surveys carried out by Passenger Focus for the Department for Transport. He added that, despite the difficulties the company faced in the early days concerning drivers' rosters, the Class 442 fleet and more recently the round of job losses in 2009, he has immense pride in the fact that South West Trains was the only TOC not to have suffered striking staff in the latest round of pay negotiations, saying that 'with Stagecoach the unions know that what you see is what you get – there are no hidden agendas'.

Throughout its franchises the company has without doubt been a well-run company under the guidance of its Chief Executive Officer Ian Dobbs (who left the company early in 2009 but, in his own words, 'on amicable terms') and Managing Director Stewart Palmer until his planned retirement in October 2009. Both men were based at the TOC's headquarters in Blackfriars Road, London, just around the corner from Southwark station. Nevertheless, as we have seen, the company has not always had a smooth ride, particularly in the early days of the new franchises. Following the departure of Ian Dobbs, Brian Souter took over the direct responsibility for the South West Trains franchise himself, telling me that he viewed his new role as an interim arrangement while he takes the opportunity to gain a better understanding of the railway and to have a chance to be involved in developing a new low-cost model for running it. Souter went on to reveal that he would also like to see a much

RIGHT: Class 442, 421/5, 455/7 and 455/8 sets stabled on Clapham Junction Traincare Depot's roads on 14 April 1996. *Brian Morrison*

RIGHT: An historic photograph taken at Bournemouth TCD shows Mark 1 heritage stock Class 423 '4-VEP' set No 3417 lined up alongside 'Desiro' Class 450 and 444 sets Nos 450001 and 444001 in what appears to have been a specially posed scenario.
Paul S. Edwards

shorter chain of command similar to that used in the bus industry.

Souter told me that without doubt 2009/10 will be a difficult time for the economy, but also dynamic for the rail industry because the railways are still fundamentally positive. He pointed to a number of things that he feels are drawing growth:

- An improved product nationwide
- It is a good way to travel – far superior to any other form of transport within the United Kingdom
- It is environmentally friendly – South West Trains has trialled a 20% bio-fuel mixture on its trains between Waterloo, Salisbury and Exeter with serious consideration being given to the use of a 100% mixture if possible
- The country's roads are becoming more and more congested.

Souter said that for 2008 and early 2009, South West Trains did not see much drainage in revenue from commuter travel, and income from season tickets had held up well, but he admits there has been some drop-off in the leisure market following the latest round of fare changes and travel time restrictions. He added that the company will have to revisit this area, and also feels that the industry will have to look at discounting to get 'lost' people back on the railway again. Stewart Palmer told me that the aims of the 2007 South West Trains winning bid had so far been achieved, but he feels that, like all Train Operators, South West Trains will find things more difficult in 2009/10 if the recession continues to bite. For South West Trains its main commercial business is London-based, and Central London employment rates are beginning to fall and are unlikely to get back to 2008 levels before 2014. Palmer explained that the overall volume of the company's services is down by around 3-4% (partly due to the drop-off in the leisure market), but by a huge 20% in business passengers travelling 1st Class. He added that those passengers are still travelling but have downgraded to Standard Class or Advance 1st, with the consequent effect on revenue from fares.

On the issue of the rail franchising system, Souter has very strong views, telling me that 'rail franchises should be at least 15 years in length but preferably 25 years, which would allow more investment'. In fact by mid-2010 further rolling-stock improvements began as SWT commenced the introduction of a rolling programme of fitting regenerative braking systems to its electric trains, (with the exception of the older Class 455 inner suburban units for which a viable financial case could not be made) making them greener and totalling around 60% of its fleet. Many of the TOCs operating electric trains use this technology and benefit from the system which

LEFT: Under threatening skies, SWT 'Desiro' Class 444 set No 444011 is pictured alongside Class 450 'Desiro' and Class 458 'Juniper' sets at Clapham Junction TCD on 13 July 2007. *Rich Mackin/ railwayscene.co.*

sees surplus electricity created under braking returned to the power supply, in SWT's case via the third rail. The first trainsets to be converted were the Class 458 'Juniper' units and by the time the upgrade is complete cost savings of around 15kWh will be made – equal to the energy needed to provide the electricity used by approximately 3,500 homes for a year. It is easy to see why the new technology is popular with environmentalists and accountants alike. SWT Engineering Director Christian Roth told *Railnews*: 'The roll out of the regenerative braking system will deliver a significant step forward in the environmental performance of our trains. We estimate that our energy consumption on the suburban network on which the Juniper units are employed will be reduced by around 8%.' South West Trains' parent company Stagecoach has a reputation for innovation and was awarded the highly sought-after 'Carbon Trust Standard' which recognised the company's attitude to climate change by measuring and reducing its carbon emissions for both its bus and rail operations. Souter concluded by saying that 'the present franchises are too prescriptive and need more flexibility'.

Whatever the effects of the 2009 recession, and whatever is still to come, the South West Trains boss made it very clear to all concerned that, unlike some franchisees, Stagecoach has absolutely no intention of handing back the keys to the franchise, and that can ultimately only be good news for South West Trains customers.

Appendix A:

The SWT driver training syllabus 2009

Basic Driver Learning – Individual Learning Plan – Version October 2009

Week Number	Day	Session 1	Session 2	Session 3	Session 4
Week 1 – Basic Rail Initial NVQ Registration and briefing	1	Introduction to Operations Training Centre Trainer and Delegate Introduction to basic driver training course	Operating Publications and equipment issue	Railway Terminology HEAD OF DRIVERS	Meet the Manager
	2	Train Crew Rosters Preparation for Duty Personal Fitness Booking on Duty	Train Crew Rosters Preparation for Duty Personal Fitness Booking on Duty	"Timetables, Diagrams" and Schedule Cards	"Timetables, Diagrams" and Schedule Cards
	3	Basic Signalling Principles	Basic Signalling Principles	Basic Signalling Principles	Basic Signalling Principles
	4	An introduction to the SWT driving policy. What makes a professional driver?	An introduction to the SWT driving policy. What makes a professional driver?	**OUT** Visit to complex station area e.g. Woking/Waterloo. Observation of railway features and an introduction to booking on point and notice/roster cases.	**OUT** Visit to complex station area e.g. Woking/Waterloo. Observation of railway features and an introduction to booking on point and notice/roster cases.
	5	Safety related communication	Operating Publications/content and Responsibility for Updating.	Lineside signs and equipment	SWT Train performance Right Time Railway
Week 2 Basic Rail	6	PERSONAL TRACK SAFETY	PERSONAL TRACK SAFETY	PERSONAL TRACK SAFETY	PERSONAL TRACK SAFETY
	7	**OUT** PERSONAL TRACK SAFETY Track walk practical Exercise/Assessment	PERSONAL TRACK SAFETY Assessment and Feedback	PERSONAL TRACK SAFETY Assessment and Feedback	PERSONAL TRACK SAFETY Summary and close
	8	**OUT** ROUTES SALOON/CAB RIDE	**OUT** ROUTES SALOON/CAB RIDE	**OUT** ROUTES SALOON/CAB RIDE	**OUT** ROUTES SALOON/CAB RIDE
	9	**OUT** VISIT to DEPOT for Introduction to Trains and Traction Units	**OUT** VISIT to DEPOT for Introduction to Trains and Traction Units	Revision of all subjects	Revision of all subjects
	10	BASIC RAIL ASSESSMENT	Basic Rail Assessment Review & Feedback	Front End Turns brief and issue of Cab Passess	Front End Turns brief and issue of Cab Passess
Week 3	11	Front End Turns	Front End Turns	Front End Turns	Front End Turns
	12	Front End Turns	Front End Turns	Front End Turns	Front End Turns
	13	Front End Turns	Front End Turns	Front End Turns	Front End Turns
	14	Front End Turns	Front End Turns	Front End Turns	Front End Turns
	15	Front End Turns	Front End Turns	Front End Turns	Front End Turns
Week 4	16	Brief review of Front End Turns – Sharing of experiences	Principles of Route Learning – Theory	Principles of Route Learning – Theory	Principles of Route Learning – Theory
	17	Principles of Route Learning **SIMULATOR**	Principles of Route Learning **SIMULATOR**	Principles of Route Learning **SIMULATOR**	Principles of Route Learning **SIMULATOR**

LEFT: Operations Trainer Jez Morgan is seen at the master console of the SWT driver training simulator at the Basingstoke-based Operations and Safety Training Centre. *John Balmforth*

BELOW LEFT: The driver training simulator cab is just like the real thing and can be set to give trainees experience of virtually any situation they may come across during the course of their careers as train drivers. The simulator can also be used to re-test experienced drivers on their periodical rules examinations. *John Balmforth*

BELOW: South West Trains driver Donna Ridgewell is seen at the controls of Class 159 set No 159105 on 3 July 2009 during a station stop at Woking. The unit was working the 09:50 Waterloo-Salisbury service. The photographer was properly authorised and supervised for a cab visit. *John Balmforth*

BOTTOM: This class of trainee drivers is undergoing instruction at the South West Trains Operations and Safety Training Centre, Basingstoke. *John Balmforth*

Week Number	Day	Session 1	Session 2	Session 3	Session 4
	18	Principles of Route Learning **SIMULATOR**	Principles of Route Learning **SIMULATOR**	Principles of Route Learning **SIMULATOR**	Principles of Route Learning **SIMULATOR**
	19	Principles of Route Learning **SIMULATOR**	Principles of Route Learning **SIMULATOR**	Principles of Route Learning **SIMULATOR**	Principles of Route Learning **SIMULATOR**
	20	Principles of Route Learning **SIMULATOR**	Principles of Route Learning **SIMULATOR**	Principles of Route Learning **SIMULATOR**	Principles of Route Learning **SIMULATOR**
Week 5 - RULES	21	Introduction to Driver's Rules Course	SWT Driver Competence Standards SC3	Rule Book Module G1 General Safety Requirements	Rule Book Module G1 General Safety Requirements
	22	Cab Secure Radio Operation. Giving & Receiving safety messages – communication protocols **SIMULATOR**	Cab Secure Radio Operation. Giving & Receiving safety messages – communication protocols **SIMULATOR**	Cab Secure Radio Operation. Giving & Receiving safety messages – communication protocols **SIMULATOR**	Cab Secure Radio Operation. Giving & Receiving safety messages – communication protocols **SIMULATOR**
	23	Rule Book Module S1 Signals & Indicators controlling train movements	Rule Book Module S1 Signals & Indicators controlling train movements	Rule Book Module S1 Signals & Indicators controlling train movements	Rule Book Module S1 Signals & Indicators controlling train movements
	24	Rule Book Module S1 Signals & Indicators	Rule Book Module S2 Observing and Obeying Fixed Signals	Rule Book Module S3 "Reporting signalling," AWS & TPWS failures and irregularities	Rule Book Module S3 "Reporting signalling," AWS & TPWS failures and irregularities
	25	**OUT** Visit to a manual signal box (e.g. Yeovil Junction or Farnham) followed by visit to a signalling centre (Eastleigh or Woking)	**OUT** Visit to a manual signal box (e.g. Yeovil Junction or Farnham) followed by visit to a signalling centre (Eastleigh or Woking)	**OUT** Visit to a manual signal box (e.g. Yeovil Junction or Farnham) followed by visit to a signalling centre (Eastleigh or Woking)	**OUT** Visit to Electrical Control Room at Eastleigh or Raynes Park
Week 6	26	**SIMULATOR** Rule Book Modules "S1, S2, S3" Signals and Indicators Observing and Obeying Fixed Signals AWS & TPWS & RT3185 Exercise	**SIMULATOR** Rule Book Modules "S1, S2, S3" Signals and Indicators Observing and Obeying Fixed Signals AWS & TPWS & RT3185 Exercise	**SIMULATOR** Rule Book Modules "S1, S2, S3" Signals and Indicators Observing and Obeying Fixed Signals AWS & TPWS & RT3185 Exercise	Revision of all Subjects
	27	Assessment No1 of all subjects	Assessment No1 of all subjects	Assessment No1 Review & Feedback	Rule Book Module S5 Passing a Signal at Danger
	28	Rule Book Module S5 Passing a Signal at Danger	Rule Book Module S5 Passing a Signal at Danger	Rule Book Module S5 Passing a Signal at Danger without authority. Driving Policy Advice on Defensive Driving and SPAD risks	Rule Book Module S4 Trains or Shunting Movements. Detained or Vehicles Left on Running Lines

Week Number	Day	Session 1	Session 2	Session 3	Session 4
	29	Rule Book Module S4 Trains or Shunting Movements. Detained or Vehicles Left on Running Lines	SIMULATOR Rule Book Modules S4 & S5 Trains or Shunting Movements. Passing a Signal at Danger Temporary Block Working	SIMULATOR Rule Book Modules S4 & S5 Trains or Shunting Movements. Passing a Signal at Danger Temporary Block Working	SIMULATOR Rule Book Modules S4 & S5 Trains or Shunting Movements. Passing a Signal at Danger Temporary Block Working
	30	Rule Book Module SS2 Shunting	Rule Book Module SS2 Shunting	**SWT Head of Operational Standards – Presentation** SPAD awareness & Professional Driving	**SWT Head of Operational Standards – Presentation** SPAD awareness & Professional Driving
Week 7	31	OUT Depot Shunting Movements Appreciation	OUT Depot Shunting Movements Appreciation	OUT Depot Shunting Movements Appreciation	Revision of all Subjects
	32	Assessment No 2 of all subjects	Assessment No 2 of all subjects	Assessment No 2 Review and Feedback	Rule Book Module SS1 Station Duties and Train Despatch
	33	Rule Book Module TW1 Preparation and Movement of Trains General	Rule Book Module TW1 Preparation and Movement of Trains General	Rule Book Module TW1 Preparation and Movement of Trains General	Rule Book Module TW1 Preparation and Movement of Trains General
	34	Rule Book Module TW2 Preparation and Movement of Multiple Unit Passenger Trains	Rule Book Module TW2 Preparation and Movement of Multiple Unit Passenger Trains	Rule Book Module TW5 Preparation and Movement of Trains – Defective or Isolated vehicles & On-Train Equipment	Rule Book Module TW5 Preparation and Movement of Trains – Defective or Isolated vehicles & On-Train Equipment
	35	Rule Book Module TW5 Preparation and Movement of Trains – Defective or Isolated vehicles & On-Train Equipment	Rule Book Module TW5 Preparation and Movement of Trains – Defective or Isolated vehicles & On-Train Equipment	Rule Book Module TW7 Wrong Direction Movements	Rule Book Module TW7 Wrong Direction Movements
Week 8	36	Rule Book Module TW8 Level Crossings	Rule Book Module TW8 Level Crossings	**SIMULATOR** Rule Book Modules TW7 & TW8 Wrong Direction Movements; Level Crossings; Interpretation of Hand Signals at Level Crossings.	**SIMULATOR** Rule Book Modules TW7 & TW8 Wrong Direction Movements; Level Crossings; Interpretation of Hand Signals at Level Crossings.
	37	Revision of all Subjects	Assessment No 3 of all Subjects	Assessment No 3 of all Subjects	Assessment No 3 Review and Feedback
	38	Rule Book Module M1 Train Stopped by "Train Accident, Fire" or Accidental Division	Rule Book Module M1 Train Stopped by "Train Accident, Fire" or Accidental Division	Rule Book Module M1 Train Stopped by "Train Accident, Fire" or Accidental Division	Rule Book Module M1 Train Stopped by "Train Accident, Fire" or Accidental Division

Week Number	Day	Session 1	Session 2	Session 3	Session 4
	39	**SIMULATOR** Rule Book Module M1 Train Accident; Emergency Call Procedure	**SIMULATOR** Rule Book Module M1 Train Accident; Emergency Call Procedure	**SIMULATOR** Rule Book Module M1 Train Accident; Emergency Call Procedure	Rule Book Module M4 Floods & Snow Rule Book Module M5 Managing Accidents
	40	Rule Book Module M2 Train Stopped by Train Failure or SWT Cut & Run Policy	Rule Book Module M2 Train Stopped by Train Failure or SWT Cut & Run Policy	**SIMULATOR** Rule Book Module M2 Train Failure and Assistance Procedures	**SIMULATOR** Rule Book Module M2 Train Failure and Assistance Procedures
Week 9	41	**SWT Fleet Representative –** Cut & Run Policy and Service Recovery Plan Briefing	**SWT Fleet Representative –** Cut & Run Policy and Service Recovery Plan Briefing	Revision of all subjects	Revision of all subjects
	42	Assessment No 4 of all subjects	Assessment No 4 of all subjects	Assessment No 4 of all subjects	Rule Book Module T11 Movement of Engineering Trains under T3 Arrangements
	43	Rule Book Module P1 Single Line Working	Rule Book Module P1 Single Line Working	**SIMULATOR** Rule Book Module P1 Single Line Working	**SIMULATOR** Rule Book Module P1 Single Line Working
	44	Rule Book Module TW6 Working Single Lines without a Train Staff or Token	Rule Book Module P2 Working of Single & Bi-Directional Lines by Pilotman	Rule Book Module SP "Permanent," Temporary and Emergency Speeds	Rule Book Module SP "Permanent," Temporary and Emergency Speeds
	45	The SWT Driving Policy – Group excercises and presentations	The SWT Driving Policy – Group excercises and presentations	The SWT Driving Policy – Group excercises and presentations	The SWT Driving Policy – Group excercises and presentations
Week 10	46	Sectional Appendix	Report writing Exercise	Revision of all subjects	Revision of all subjects
	47	Assessment No5 of all subjects	Assessment No5 of all subjects	Assessment No 5 Review & Feedback	DC Electrified Lines & Short Circuit Bar
	48	DC Electrified Lines & Short Circuit Bar	**OUT** Short Circuiting Bar and on train emergency evacuation practical session at Barton Mill	**OUT** Short Circuiting Bar and on train emergency evacuation practical session at Barton Mill	**OUT** Short Circuiting Bar and on train emergency evacuation practical session at Barton Mill
	49	**SIMULATOR** Driving in Adverse Weather Conditions	**SIMULATOR** Driving in Adverse Weather Conditions	**SIMULATOR** Driving in Adverse Weather Conditions	**SIMULATOR** Driving in Adverse Weather Conditions
	50	Revision of all subjects	Revision of all subjects	Revision of all subjects	Revision of all subjects
Week 11	51	**Driver's Rules Final Assessment**	**Driver's Rules Final Assessment**	**Driver's Rules Final Assessment**	**Driver's Rules Final Assessment Review & Feedback**
Interim NVQ Review	52	Introduction to SWT Traction. Basic Electricity/Diesel	Introduction to SWT Traction. Basic Electricity/Diesel	Introduction to SWT Traction. Basic Electricity/Diesel	Introduction to SWT Traction. Basic Electricity/Diesel

Week Number	Day	Session 1	Session 2	Session 3	Session 4
	53	Depot Driving Slow Speed Movements	Depot Driving Slow Speed Movements	Depot Driving Slow Speed Movements	Depot Driving Slow Speed Movements
	54	Depot Driving Slow Speed Movements	Depot Driving Slow Speed Movements	Depot Driving Slow Speed Movements	Depot Driving Slow Speed Movements
	55	Depot Driving Slow Speed Movements	Depot Driving Slow Speed Movements	Depot Driving Slow Speed Movements	Depot Driving Slow Speed Movements
Week 12	56	Training Train/ Service Train Traction Specific	Training Train/ Service Train Traction Specific	Training Train/ Service Train Traction Specific	Training Train/ Service Train Traction Specific
	57	Training Train/ Service Train Traction Specific	Training Train/ Service Train Traction Specific	Training Train/ Service Train Traction Specific	Training Train/ Service Train Traction Specific
	58	Training Train/ Service Train Traction Specific	Training Train/ Service Train Traction Specific	Training Train/ Service Train Traction Specific	Training Train/ Service Train Traction Specific
	59	Training Train/ Service Train Traction Specific	Training Train/ Service Train Traction Specific	Training Train/ Service Train Traction Specific	Training Train/ Service Train Traction Specific
	60	Training Train/ Service Train Traction Specific	Training Train/ Service Train Traction Specific	Training Train/ Service Train Traction Specific	Training Train/ Service Train Traction Specific
Week 13	61	Training Train/ Service Train Traction Specific	Training Train/ Service Train Traction Specific	Training Train/ Service Train Traction Specific	Training Train/ Service Train Traction Specific
	62	Training Train/ Service Train Traction Specific	Training Train/ Service Train Traction Specific	Training Train/ Service Train Traction Specific	Training Train/ Service Train Traction Specific
	63	Training Train/ Service Train Traction Specific	Training Train/ Service Train Traction Specific	Training Train/ Service Train Traction Specific	Training Train/ Service Train Traction Specific
	64	Training Train/ Service Train Traction Specific	Training Train/ Service Train Traction Specific	Training Train/ Service Train Traction Specific	Training Train/ Service Train Traction Specific
	65	Training Train/ Service Train Traction Specific	Training Train/ Service Train Traction Specific	Training Train/ Service Train Traction Specific	Training Train/ Service Train Traction Specific
Week 14	66	Training Train/ Service Train Traction Specific	Training Train/ Service Train Traction Specific	Training Train/ Service Train Traction Specific	Training Train/ Service Train Traction Specific
	67	Training Train/ Service Train Traction Specific	Training Train/ Service Train Traction Specific	Training Train/ Service Train Traction Specific	Training Train/ Service Train Traction Specific
	68	ANNUAL LEAVE	ANNUAL LEAVE	ANNUAL LEAVE	ANNUAL LEAVE
	69	ANNUAL LEAVE	ANNUAL LEAVE	ANNUAL LEAVE	ANNUAL LEAVE
	70	ANNUAL LEAVE	ANNUAL LEAVE	ANNUAL LEAVE	ANNUAL LEAVE
Week 15	71	ANNUAL LEAVE	ANNUAL LEAVE	ANNUAL LEAVE	ANNUAL LEAVE
	72	ANNUAL LEAVE	ANNUAL LEAVE	ANNUAL LEAVE	ANNUAL LEAVE
Weeks 16-22 (approximately)	73	Practical Handling with a Driver Instructor for approx 7 weeks	Practical Handling with a Driver Instructor for approx 7 weeks	Practical Handling with a Driver Instructor for approx 7 weeks	Practical Handling with a Driver Instructor for approx 7 weeks

Week Number	Day	Session 1	Session 2	Session 3	Session 4
Week 23 (approximately) Mid NVQ Review	n/a	Revision of key points of PRL previously learnt and discussion about route experiences gained from initial period with DI. Introduction and brief of route learning exercise over core route	Revision of key points of PRL previously learnt and discussion about route experiences gained from initial period with DI. Introduction and brief of route learning exercise over core route	OUT Route Learning Exercise over Core Route.	OUT Route Learning Exercise over Core Route.
		OUT Route Learning Exercise over Core Route.	**OUT** Route Learning Exercise over Core Route.	**OUT** Route Learning Exercise over Core Route.	**OUT** Route Learning Exercise over Core Route.
		OUT Route Learning Exercise over Core Route.	**OUT** Route Learning Exercise over Core Route.	**OUT** Route Learning Exercise over Core Route.	**OUT** Route Learning Exercise over Core Route.
		OUT Route Learning Exercise over Core Route.	**OUT** Route Learning Exercise over Core Route.	**OUT** Route Learning Exercise over Core Route.	**OUT** Route Learning Exercise over Core Route.
		OUT Route Learning Exercise over Core Route.	**OUT** Route Learning Exercise over Core Route.	**OUT** Route Learning Exercise over Core Route.	**OUT** Route Learning Exercise over Core Route.
Week 24 (approximately)	n/a	Traction Course 455/159	Traction Course 455/159	Traction Course 455/159	Traction Course 455/159
		Traction Course 455/442	Traction Course 455/159	Traction Course 455/159	Traction Course 455/159
		Traction Course 455/442	Traction Course 455/159	Traction Course 455/159	Traction Course 455/159
		Traction Course 455/442	Traction Course 455/159	Traction Course 455/159	Traction Course 455/159
		Traction Course 455/442	Traction Course 455/159	Traction Course 455/159	Traction Course 455/159
Week 25 (approximately)	n/a	Traction Course 455/442	Traction Course 455/159	Traction Course 455/159	Traction Course 455/159
		Traction Course 455/442	Traction Course 455/159	Traction Course 455/159	Traction Course 455/159
		Traction ASSESSMENT 455/159	**Traction ASSESSMENT 455/159**	**Traction ASSESSMENT 455/159**	**Traction ASSESSMENT 455/159**
		Traction ASSESSMENT 455/159	**Traction ASSESSMENT 455/159**	**Traction ASSESSMENT 455/159**	**Traction ASSESSMENT 455/159**
		Traction Course 444/450 Desiro	Traction Course 444/450 Desiro	Traction Course 444/450 Desiro	Traction Course 444/450 Desiro

Week Number	Day	Session 1	Session 2	Session 3	Session 4
Week 26 (approximately)	n/a	Traction Course 444/450 Desiro	Traction Course 444/450 Desiro	Traction Course 444/450 Desiro	Traction Course 444/450 Desiro
		Traction Course 444/450 Desiro	Traction Course 444/450 Desiro	Traction Course 444/450 Desiro	Traction Course 444/450 Desiro
		Traction Course 444/450 Desiro	Traction Course 444/450 Desiro	Traction Course 444/450 Desiro	Traction Course 444/450 Desiro
		Traction Course 444/450 Desiro	Traction Course 444/450 Desiro	Traction Course 444/450 Desiro	Traction Course 444/450 Desiro
		Traction Course 444/450 Desiro	Traction Course 444/450 Desiro	Traction Course 444/450 Desiro	Traction Course 444/450 Desiro
Week 27 (approximately)	n/a	Traction Course 444/450 Desiro	Traction Course 444/450 Desiro	Traction Course 444/450 Desiro	Traction Course 444/450 Desiro
		Traction ASSESSMENT 444/450	**Traction ASSESSMENT 444/450**	**Traction ASSESSMENT 444/450**	**Traction ASSESSMENT 444/450**
		Traction ASSESSMENT 444/450	**Traction ASSESSMENT 444/450**	**Traction ASSESSMENT 444/450**	**Traction ASSESSMENT 444/450**
		ANNUAL LEAVE	ANNUAL LEAVE	ANNUAL LEAVE	ANNUAL LEAVE
		ANNUAL LEAVE	ANNUAL LEAVE	ANNUAL LEAVE	ANNUAL LEAVE
Week 28 (approximately)	n/a	ANNUAL LEAVE	ANNUAL LEAVE	ANNUAL LEAVE	ANNUAL LEAVE
		ANNUAL LEAVE	ANNUAL LEAVE	ANNUAL LEAVE	ANNUAL LEAVE
		ANNUAL LEAVE	ANNUAL LEAVE	ANNUAL LEAVE	ANNUAL LEAVE
Weeks 29-38 (approximately) Interim NVQ review approximately week 33	n/a	Practical Handling with a Driver Instructor for approximately 9 weeks.	Practical Handling with a Driver Instructor for approximately 9 weeks.	Practical Handling with a Driver Instructor for approximately 9 weeks.	Practical Handling with a Driver Instructor for approximately 9 weeks.
Final NVQ Review	n/a	**FINAL ASSESSMENT OF COMPETENCE**	**FINAL ASSESSMENT OF COMPETENCE**	**FINAL ASSESSMENT OF COMPETENCE**	**FINAL ASSESSMENT OF COMPETENCE**

Candidate's Signature .... Date ....

Assessor's Signature .... Date ....

Appendix B

The South West Trains fleet – TECHNICAL DETAILS

CLASS 158 DMU TECHNICAL DATA

Sub Class used by SWT	**158/0**
Number range	158880-158890 (11 units)
Introduced	1989-1992
Built by	BREL, Derby
Formation	DMSL(A) + DMCL
Vehicle numbers	
DMSL(A)	57880-57890,
DMCL	52880-52890
Vehicle length	76ft 1¾in (23.21m)
Height	12ft 6in (3.81m)
Width	9ft 3¼in (2.82m)
Seating	Total 127 seats (13 1st Class, 114 Standard Class);
DMSL(A)	64 Standard Class,
DMCL	13 1st Class, 50 Standard Class
Internal layout	2+2 Standard Class, 2+1 1st Class
Gangway	Throughout
Toilet	DMCL 1
Weight	Total 77 tonnes;
DMSL(A)	38.5 tonnes,
DMCL	38.5 tonnes
Brake type	Air/electro-pneumatic
Bogie type	
Powered vehicle,	BREL P4;
Trailer vehicle,	BREL T4
Power unit	NT855R 350hp (261kW), one per vehicle
Transmission	Hydraulic
Transmission type	Voith T211r
Horsepower (total)	700hp (522kW)
Maximum speed	90mph (145kph)
Coupling type	BSI
Multiple restriction	Classes 14x, 15x, 17x
Door type	Bi-parting sliding plug
Special features	Radio Electric Token Block (RETB) ready
Body structure	Aluminium
Owner	Porterbrook

Source: *Traction Recognition* and *Rail Guide 2010* by Colin J. Marsden (2007/2010, Ian Allan Publishing Ltd)

CLASS 159 DMU TECHNICAL DATA

Sub-Class	**159/0**	**159/1**
Number range	159001-159022	159101-159109
Introduced	1992-1993	1991 (intended to be Class 158s), 2006
Built by	BREL, Derby, fitted out by Rosyth Dockyard, Scotland	BREL, Derby, rebuilt at Wabtec, Doncaster
Formation	DMCL+MSL+DMSL	DMCL+MSL+DMSL
Vehicle numbers	DMCL 52873/52894 MSL 58718/58739 DMSL 57873/57894	DMCL 52800/52814 range MSL 58701/58717 range DMSL 57800/57814 range
Vehicle length	76ft 1¾in (23.21m)	76ft 1¾in (23.21m)
Height	12ft 6in (3.81m)	12ft 6in (3.81m)
Width	9ft 3¼in (2.82m)	9ft 3¼in (2.82m)

	159/0	159/1
Seating	24 1st Class, 172 Standard Class	24 1st Class, 170 Standard Class
DCML	24 1st Class, 28 Standard Class	24 1st Class, 28 Standard Class
MSL	72 Standard Class	70 Standard Class
DMSL	72 Standard Class	72 Standard Class
Internal layout	2+1 1st Class, 2+2 Standard Class	2+1 1st Class, 2+2 Standard Class
Gangway	Throughout	Throughout
Toilets	DCML 1, DMSL 1, MSL 1	DCML 1, DMSL 1, MSL 1
Weight		
DCML	38.5 tonnes	38.5 tonnes
MSL	38 tonnes	38 tonnes
DMSL	37.8 tonnes	37.8 tonnes
Brake type	Air/electro-pneumatic	Air/electro-pneumatic
Bogie type		
Powered vehicle	BREL P4-4	BREL P4-4
Trailer vehicle	BREL T4-4	BREL T4-4
Power Unit	Cummins NTA855R One per vehicle	Cummins NTA855R One per vehicle
Transmission	Hydraulic	Hydraulic
Transmission type	Voith T211r	Voith T211r
Horsepower (total)	1,200hp (895kW)	1,200hp (895kW)
Maximum speed	90mph (145kph)	90mph (145kph)
Coupling type	BSI	BSI
Multiple restriction	14x, 15x, 170 series	14x, 15x, 170 series
Door type	Bi-parting swing plug	Bi-parting swing plug
Body structure	Aluminium	
Owner	Porterbrook	

Still in service with SWT

159/0	22
159/1	1

Named Units

159001	'City of Exeter'
159002	'City of Salisbury'
159003	'Templecombe'
159004	'Basingstoke and Deane'

Source: *Traction Recognition* and *Rail Guide 2010* by Colin J. Marsden (2007/2010, Ian Allan Publishing Ltd)

ABOVE: The 10:02 SWT service from Paignton to Brighton and Portsmouth Harbour departs from Dawlish on 1 September 2007, formed of Class 159/1 set No 159101 and Class 159/0 set No 159012. *Brian Morrison*

LEFT: Class 159 sets Nos 159001 and 159010 are seen approaching Dawlish on 15 July 2006, forming the 10:07 South West Trains summer Saturday service from Paignton to Brighton. *Colin J. Marsden*

CLASS 421 '3-CIG' EMUs TECHNICAL DATA

Sub Class	**421/7**
Number range	1392 withdrawn 2005 1497 'Freshwater' - previously 1883 1498 'Farringford' - previously 1888
Alpha Code	3-CIG (3-car Corridor Intermediate Guards)
Built	1971 - built by BREL, York as 4-car '4-CIG' sets
Modified to 3-CIG	2004 by SWT Wimbledon Traincare Depot
Formation	DTCOL(A)+MBS+DTSOL(B)
Vehicle numbers	
DTCOL(A)	76470*, 76764, 76773
MBS	62378*, 62402, 62411
DTSOL(B)	76811*, 76835, 76844 * withdrawn 2005
Vehicle length	64ft 9½in (19.75m)
Height	12ft 9¼in (3.89m)
Width	9ft 3in (2.81m)
Seating	
DTCOL(A)	18 First 36 Standard
MBS	56 Standard
DTSOL(B)	54 Standard
Internal layout	6 seat compartments in First, 2+2 in Standard
Gangway	Throughout
Toilets	DTSOL(B) - 2 fitted
Weight	
DTCOL(A)	35.5 tonnes
MBS	49 tonnes
DTCOL(B)	35 tonnes
Brake type	Air (Auto/Electro Pneumatic)
Bogie Type	
Power vehicle	Mk6
Trailer vehicle	B5 (SR)
Power collection	750V dc third rail
Traction motor type	4 x EE507
Horsepower	1,000hp (740kW)
Maximum Speed	90mph (145kph) - restricted to 40mph on Lymington Branch
Coupling type	Buck-eye
Multiple restriction	1951-1966 SR stock, 73/1, 33/1
Door type	Slam - Central Door Locking fitted at modification
Total No of Sets	2
Body construction	Steel
Owner	Stagecoach South West Trains Ltd
Route	Brockenhurst - Lymington Pier shuttle

Source: *Traction Recognition* and *Rail Guide 2010* by Colin J. Marsden (2007/2010, Ian Allan Publishing Ltd)
www.therailwaycentre.com/Recognition

CLASSES 444 AND 450 EMUs TECHNICAL DATA

Class	**444**	**450/0 & 450/5**
Number range	444001-444045	450001-450-127
Introduced	2003-2005	2002-2007
Built by	Siemens Transportation SGP, Austria	Siemens Duewag, Germany and Siemens Transportation SGP, Austria
Formation	5-car DMSO+TSO(A)+ TSO(B)+TSRMB+ DMCO	4-car DMOS(A)+TCO+TSO+ DMOS(B)
Vehicle numbers		
DMSO	63801-63845	
TSO(A)	67101-67145	
TSO(B)	67151-67195	
TSRMB	67201-67245	
DMCO	63851-63895	
DMOS(A)		63201-63300 / 63701-63710 / 63901-63917
TCO		64201-64300 / 66851-66860 / 63921-63937
TSO		68101-68200 / 66801-66810 / 66901-66917
DMOS(B)		63601-63700 / 63751-63760 / 66921-66937
Vehicle length	77ft 3in (23.57m)	66ft 9in (20.4m)
Height	12ft 1½in (3.7m)	12ft 1½in (3.7m)
Width	8ft 9in (2.74m)	9ft 2in (2.8m
Seating		
DMSO / DMOS(A)	76 Standard	70 Standard
TSO(A) / TCO	76 Standard	24 First 36 Standard
TSO(B) / TSO	76 Standard	70 Standard
TSRMB / DMOS(B)	47 Standard	79 Standard
DMCO	35 First 24 Standard	

LEFT: The 16:00 SWT service from Weymouth to London Waterloo arrives at Wool on 12 May 2007, formed by Class 444 'Desiro' set No 444017. *Brian Morrison*

	444	450/0 & 450/5
Internal layout	2+2 Standard 2+1 First	2+3 Standard 2+2 First
Gangway	Throughout	Throughout
Toilets	TSO-1, TSRMB-1	TCO-1, TSO-1
Weight		
DMSO / DMOS(A)	52 tonnes	46 tonnes
TSO(A) / TCO	41 tonnes	35 tonnes
TSO(B) / TSO	37 tonnes	35 tonnes
TSRMB / DMOS(B)	42 tonnes	46 tonnes
DMCO	52 tonnes	
Brake type	Air / Regenerative	Air / Regenerative
Bogie type	Siemens SGB5000	Siemens SGB/SF5000
Power collection	750V dc third rail	750V dc third rail
Traction type	1 TB2016 three phase	4 x 1TB2016 0GB02 three phase
Output	2,682hp (2,000kW)	2,682hp (2,000kW)
Maximum speed	100mph (161kph)	100mph (161kph)
Coupling type:		
Outer	Dellner 12	Dellner 12
Inner	semi-auto	semi-auto
Multiple restrictions	Classes 444 / 450	Classes 444 / 450
Door type	Single leaf sliding plug	Bi-parting sliding plug
Body construction	Aluminium	Aluminium
Special features	Air Conditioning Passenger Information System and CCTV	Air Conditioning Passenger Information System and CCTV
Owner	Angel Trains	Angel Trains
No in service	45	99 / 28
Named Sets	444001 'Naomi House' 444002 'Destination Weymouth' 444018 'FAB 444'	450015 'Desiro' 450042 'Treloar College' 450114 'FAIRBRIDGE - investing in the future

Source: *Traction Recognition* and *Rail Guide 2010* by Colin J. Marsden (2007/2010, Ian Allan Publishing Ltd)

CLASS 455 SERIES EMUs TECHNICAL DATA

Sub-class	455/7	455/8	455/9
Number range	455701-455742/50	455847-455874	455901-455920
Built by	BREL, York	BREL, York	BREL, York
Introduced	1984-85	1982-84	1985
Refurbished	2003-07 by Bombardier at Chart Leacon	2003-08 by Bombardier at Chart Leacon	2004-07 by Bombardier at Chart Leacon
Formation	4-car DTSO(A)+MSO+TSO+ DTSO(B)	4-car DTSO(A)+MSO+TSO+ DTSO(B)	4-car DTSO(A)+MSO+TSO+ DTSO(B)
Vehicle numbers			
DTSO(A)	77727-77811 odd Nos	77579-77725 odd Nos	77813-77852 odd Nos
MSO	62783-62825	62709-62782	62826-62845
TSO	71526-71568	71637-71710	71714-71733
DTSO(B)	77728-77812 odd Nos	77580-77726 odd Nos	77814-77852 odd Nos
Vehicle length			
DTSO(A) & DTSO(B)	65ft 0½in (19.83m)	65ft 0½in (19.83m)	65ft 0½in (19.83m)
MSO	65ft 4½in (19.91m)	65ft 4½in (19.91m)	65ft 4½in (19.91m)
TSO	65ft 4½in (19.91m)	65ft 4½in (19.91m)	65ft 4½in (19.91m)

	455/7	455/8	455/9
Height			
DTSO(A) & DTSO(B)	12ft 1½in (3.7m)	12ft 1½in (3.7m)	12ft 1½in (3.7m)
MSO	12ft 1½in (3.7m)	12ft 1½in (3.7m)	12ft 1½in (3.7m)
TSO	12ft 1½in (3.7m)	12ft 1½in (3.7m)	12ft 1½in (3.7m)
ex Class 508 car	11ft 6½in (3.58m)		
Width	9ft 3¼in (2.82m)	9ft 3¼in (2.82m)	9ft 3¼in (2.82m)
Seating:			
DTSO(A) & DTSO(B)	54 Standard	74 Standard	54 Standard
MSO	68 Standard	84 Standard	68 Standard
TSO	68 Standard	84 Standard	68 Standard
Internal layout	2+2	2+3	2+2
Gangway	Throughout	Throughout	Throughout
Toilets	None fitted	None fitted	None fitted
Weight			
DTSO(A) & DTSO(B)	29.5 tonnes	29.5 tonnes	29 tonnes
MSO	45.5 tonnes	50 tonnes	45.5 tonnes
TSO	25.5 tonnes	28.1 tonnes	27.1 tonnes
Brake type	Air (Westcode)	Air (Westcode)	Air (Westcode)
Bogie type			
DTSO(A) & DTSO(B)	BREL BT13	BREL BT13	BREL BT13
MSO	BREL P27	BREL P20	BREL P20
TSO	BREL BX1	BREL BT13	BREL BT13
Power collection	750V dc third rail	750V dc third rail	750V dc third rail
Traction Motor type	4 x EE507	4 x EE507	4 x EE507
Horsepower	1,000hp (746kW)	1,000hp (746kW)	1,000hp (746kW)
Maximum Speed	75mph (121kph)	75mph (121kph)	75mph (121kph)
Coupling type			
Outer	tightlock	tightlock	tightlock
Inner	bar	bar	bar
Multiple restrictions	Classes 455/456	Classes 455/456	Classes 455/456
Door type	Bi-parting sliding	Bi-parting sliding	Bi-parting sliding
Special features	CCTV	CCTV	CCTV
Body construction			
DTSO(A) & DTSO(B) & MSO	Steel	Steel	Steel
TSO	Aluminium		
In service with SWT	43	74	20
Owner	Porterbrook	Porterbrook	Porterbrook

Source: *Traction Recognition* by Colin J. Marsden (December 2007, Ian Allan Publishing Ltd)

LEFT: Class 455/9 EMU sets Nos 5914 and 5913 await departure from Waterloo on 2 December 2008, forming respectively the 17:52 service to Weybridge via Richmond and the 18:02 to Guildford via Surbiton. *Brian Morrison*

RIGHT: Awaiting their next turns of duty at Waterloo in April 2009 are Class 455 sets Nos 5729 and 5867 alongside Class 458 'Juniper' set No 8019. The roof of the currently disused former Eurostar terminal can also be seen to the left of the trains. *John Balmforth*

CLASS 458 EMUs TECHNICAL DATA

Number range	458001-458030
Alpha code	4-JOP (4-car Juniper Outer Suburban owned by Porterbrook)
Introduced	1999-2002
Formation	DMCO(A)+PTSO+MSO+DMCO(B)
Vehicle numbers	
DMCO(A)	67601-67630
PTSO	74001-74030
MSO	74101-74130
DMCO(B)	67701-67730
Vehicle length	
DMCO(A) & DMCO(B)	69ft 6in (21.16m)
PTSO & MSO	65ft 4in (19.94m)
Height	12ft 3in (3.77m)
Width	9ft 2in (2.80m)
Seating	
DMCO(A) & DMCO(B)	12 First 63 Standard
PTSO	49 Standard
MSO	75 Standard
Internal layout	2+2 First, 2+3 Standard
Gangway	Throughout
Toilets	PTSO-1
Weight	
DMCO(A) & DMCO(B)	45.2 tonnes
PTSO	33.3 tonnes
MOS	40.6 tonnes
Brake type	Air / Regenerative
Bogie type	ACR
Power collection	750V dc third rail
Traction Motor type	6 x Alstom
Horsepower	2,172hp (1,620kW)
Maximum Speed	100mph (161kph)
Coupling type	
Outer	tightlock
Inner	semi-auto
Multiple restrictions	Class 458 only
Door type	Bi-parting sliding plug
Special features	Air Conditioning, Electronic Passenger Information System
Total No of Sets	30 - (all in service with South West Trains)
Body construction	Steel
Owner	Porterbrook
Note	4-JOP also known as 4-car Juniper Open Plan

Source: *Traction Recognition* by Colin J. Marsden (December 2007, Ian Allan Publishing Ltd)

CLASS 483 EMUs TECHNICAL DATA

(ex London Underground stock – units used on Island Line services)

Number Range	483002 / 483004 / 483006 483007 / 483008 / 403009
Introduced to:	
London Transport	1938
Isle of Wight	1988/90
Built by	Metro-Cammell
Rebuilt by	BREL, Eastleigh
Formation	2-car DMSO(A)+DMSO(B)
Vehicle numbers:	
DMSO(A)	122 / 124 / 126 / 127 / 128 / 129
DMSO(B)	222 / 224 / 226 / 227 / 228 / 229
Vehicle lengths	
DMSO(A) & DMSO(B)	52ft 4in (15.95m)
Height	9ft 5½in (2.88m)

Width	8ft 8½in (2.65m)
Seating	
DMSO(A)	40 Standard
DMSO(B)	42 Standard
Internal layout	2+2 plus bench seats
Gangway	Within set, plus emergency end doors
Toilets	None fitted
Weight	
DMSO(A) & DMSO(B)	27.4 tonnes
Brake type	Air (Auto/EP)
Bogie type	London Transport
Power collection	660V dc third rail
Traction Motor type	4 x Crompton Parkinson / GEC / BTH
Horsepower	670hp (500kW)
Maximum Speed	45mph (72.5kph)
Coupling type	Wedgelock
Multiple restrictions	Class 483 only
Door type	Bi-parting and single sliding
No of sets available	6 - normally only 4 in use
Body construction	Steel
Owner	Stagecoach South Western Trains Ltd

Source: *Traction Recognition* by Colin J. Marsden (2007, Ian Allan Publishing Ltd)

ABOVE: The driver's cab and controls of Island Line Class 483 set No 007. *John Balmforth*

BELOW: For the enthusiast, nostalgia abounds in this view of the guard's door and emergency controls of Class 483 set No 008. *John Balmforth*

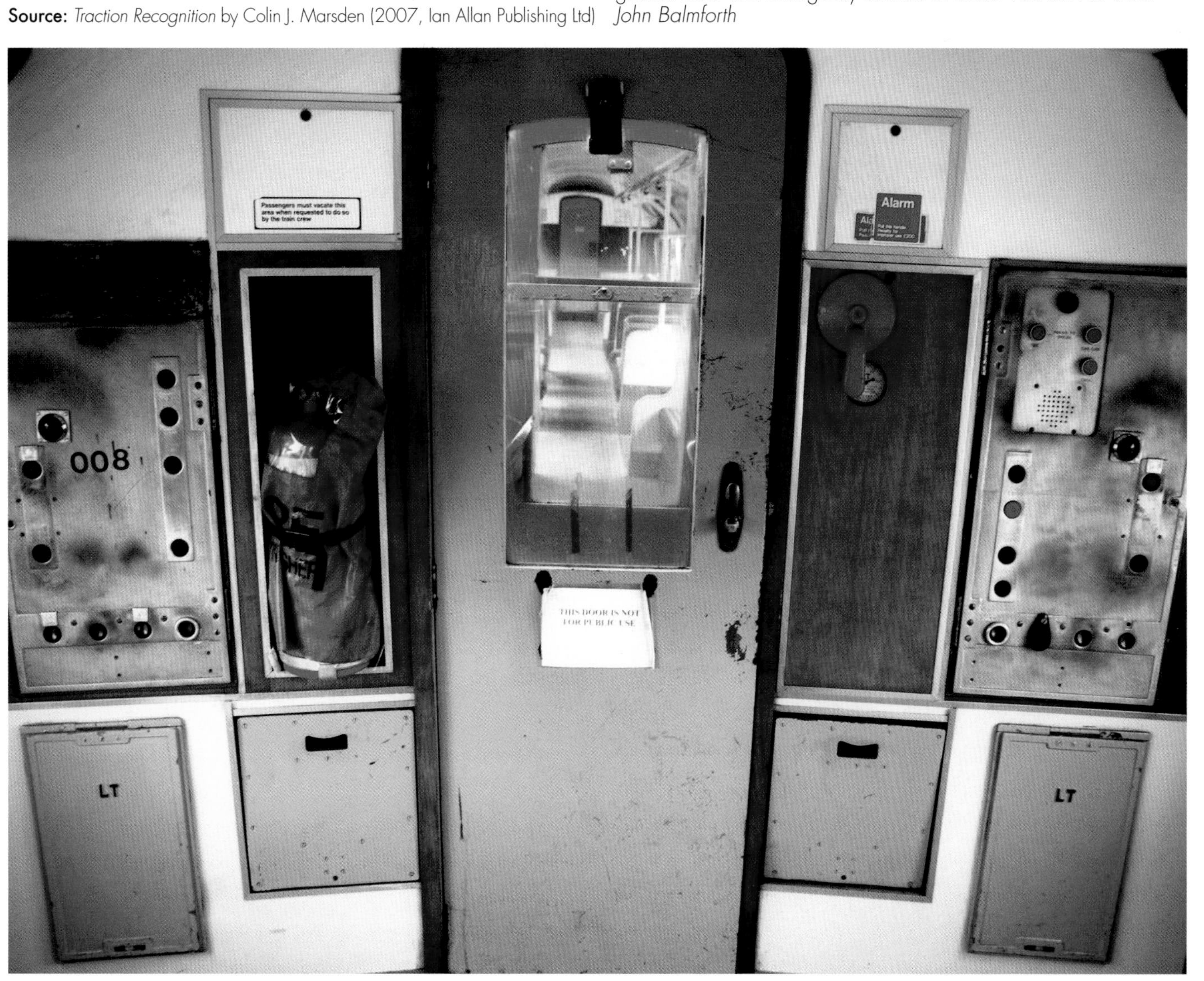

Appendix C

Interesting facts and figures

Franchise subsidy/premium profile in £millions – new franchise awarded 2007

2006/07	+£16.3
2007/08	+£63.6
2008/09	+£25.0
2009/10	-£40.7
2010/11	-£85.8
2011/12	-£140.0
2012/13	-£197.6
2013/14	-£247.9
2014/15	-£295.7
2015/16	-£342.8
2016/17	-£331.5

Notes: 2006/07 represents only part year ended 31 March 2007 due to award of new franchise. 2016/17 represents part year ended 4 February 2017 when franchise ends. Amounts are calculated at 2006/07 prices

Source: Department of Transport, Franchise payment profiles 19 May 2009

South West Trains operating profit in £millions, franchise ended 3 February 2007,

1995/96	£1.4
1996/97	£6.3
1997/98	£21.2
1998/99	£33.1
1999/00	£37.1
2000/01	£47.1
2001/02	£32.2
2002/03	£40.8
2003/04	£43.6
2004/05	£48.8
2005/06	£61.9
2006/07	£47.9

Note: 2006/07 reflects franchise ending 4 February 2007

Source: Department of Transport, Franchise payment profiles 19 May 2009

South West Trains turnover in £millions franchise 4 February 1996-3 February 2007

1996/97	£283.4
1997/98	£316.7
1998/99	£336.2
1999/00	£364.8
2000/01	£395.7
2001/02	£394.2
2002/03	£404.82
2003/04	£433.79
2004/05	£467.4
2005/06	£493.8
2006/07	£557.3

Source: Stagecoach/South West Trains and South West Trains Statutory Accounts,courtesy of Andy West, South West Trains Finance Director, September 2009

Total number of passenger journeys made on South West Trains services (in millions) during franchise ended 3rd February 2007

2000/01	142
2001/02	138
2002/03	141
2003/04	143
2004/05	151
2005/06	160
2006/07	175

South West Trains carries approximately 400,000 passengers each day, with between 250,000 and 300,000 travelling through Waterloo station, of whom at least 100,000 do so in the morning peak.

Source: Stagecoach/South West Trains

Total number of train services operated by South West Trains

Trains per week

Year	Number
1996	10,000
2002	10,992
2005	11,088
2008	10,952

Trains per day

Monday-Friday	8,375
Saturday	1,563
Sunday	1,014
Total per week	**10,952**

SWT services into Waterloo during morning peak

07:00-10:00	151

Distance covered

Non-electrified route miles	192
Electrified route miles	424
Total route miles	**616**

Source: Stagecoach/South West Trains

General information about South West Trains

Staff employed (2009, including 39 at Island Line)	5,201
Train drivers	1,234
Train guards	831
Ticket office/platform staff	1,205
Train presentation	188
Automatic barriers	19
CCTV cameras	2,100
Pan tilt zoom cameras	72
Linked stations	73
Stations managed by SWT	177
Stations served by SWT	215
Full maintenance depots	5
Secure Station awards won	69
Car parks managed and operated by SWT	156
Spaces in SWT-operated car parks	18,516

Source: Stagecoach/South West Trains

Appendix D

Island Line Passengers Carried Year-by-Year

Year	Ryde Pier Head	Ryde Esplanade	Ryde St John's Road	Smallbrook Junction	Brading	Sandown	Lake	Shanklin
2004/05	121,387	453,000*	160,891	3,087	66,932	243,000*	77,995	342,000*
2005/06	116,812	457,000*	175,208	2,716	69,074	254,000*	76,364	345,000*
2006/07	149,226	489,000*	178,869	2,965	68,841	265,000*	71,465	383,000*
SWT Franchise								
2007/08	120,181	443,000*	178,914	4,363	60,680	265,000*	69,350	369,000*
2008/09	127,514	397,715	190,956	4,458	65,851	264,952	67,316	364,224

* exact numbers not available but are Island Line's own estimate
Pre-SWT franchise figures included for comparison purposes

Source: *Island Line (part of Stagecoach South Western Trains Ltd)*

Appendix E

South West Trains Traincare Depots, Traincare Facilities and Berthing Sidings

Location	Depot code	Classes maintained
Barton Mill, Basingstoke (Berthing siding only)	XBS	158/159/444/450
Bournemouth Traincare Depot	BM	73/158/159/421/444/450/455
Clapham Junction TCD	CLY	444/450/455/458
Farnham TCD	XFN	444/450
Fratton, Portsmouth TCD	FR	444/450
Northam, Southampton TCD	NT	444/450
Portsmouth Harbour (berthing siding only)	PMH	444/450
Ryde St John's Road TCD, Ryde, Isle of Wight	RY	483
Salisbury Traincare Depot (Diesel)	SA	158/159
Southsea Low Level, Portsmouth, Down Carriage Sidings (DCS) (berthing siding only)	PMS	444/450
Strawberry Hill, Twickenham (Traincare facility)	VZ	450/455
East Wimbledon Traincare Depot	WD	444/450/455/458

South West Trains rolling stock can also be seen at other locations on the network, but these are normally only used for the stabling of trains between services.

RIGHT: South West Trains 'Desiro' set No 444039 is caught by the photographer on the lifting jacks at Bournemouth TCD after having its bogies removed for maintenance. *Paul S. Edwards*

ABOVE: Night-time shots of the railway are always special. Here we see SWT 'Desiro' Class 450 set No 450087 stabled at Clapham TCD after finishing its day's work in November 2004. In the background a Class 421 slam-door heritage set is just visible. *South West Trains Picture Library*

BELOW: Clapham Yard on 5 December 2001, showing (left to right) Class 455/8 set No 5804, 'Queen of Scots' stock, Class 423/1 '4-VEP' set No 3549, and Class 450 'Desiro' set No 450029. *Brian Morrison*

OPPOSITE: One of South West Trains' Class 455/7 EMUs, painted in the company's bright red inner-suburban livery, is caught on camera inside Wimbledon Park Traincare Depot as it awaits its next turn of duty. *South West Trains Picture Library*

Bibliography

Hardy, Brian; *Tube Trains on the Isle of Wight* (Harrow Weald: Capital Transport Publishing, 2003)

Jack, Doug; *Twenty-Five Years of Stagecoach* (Hersham: Ian Allan Publishing Ltd, 2005)

Johnston, Howard (Ed); *The Comprehensive Guide to Britain's Railways* (Peterborough: EMAP Active Ltd; 7th ed 2004, 8th ed 2005, 10th ed 2007)

Johnston, Howard and Harris, Ken; *Jane's Train Recognition Guide* (London: Collins, 2005)

Marsden, Colin J. (Ed); *Modern Locomotives Illustrated* No 178 'Desiro' EMUs August 2009-September 2009 (pp7, 8, 10, 15, 70-71, 74-75) (Dawlish)

Silvester, Katie (Ed); *Rail Professional*, issue 152, November 2009 p11 (Cambridge: Cambridge Publishers Ltd)

Wolmar, Christian; *Stagecoach: A Classic Rags-to-Riches Tale From The Frontiers Of Capitalism* (London: Orion Business Books, 1999)

Internet sites

www.guardian.co.uk/business2009, pp1-3 (accessed 25/06/2009)

www.networkrail.co.uk/aspx/959.aspx#maps (re Waterloo station; accessed 02/04/2009)

www.therailwaycentre.com *Bio fuel trials for SWT Class 159* (accessed 21/10/2009)

www.southwesttrains.co.uk Aboutus/Corporate+Information (accessed 22/12/2008);
Group Structure (accessed 22/12/2008);
Facts and figures (accessed 22/12/2008);
SWtrains/TravelInformation/ourFleetofTrains (accessed 22/12/2008)

www.stagecoachgroup.com media/contacts (accessed 22/12/2008);
Group structure (accessed 30/12/2008);
Rail Franchise bids (accessed 22/12/2008);
Key Facts (accessed 30/12/2008);
Performance Indicators (accessed 30/12/2008)

http://en.wikipedia.org/wiki/South West Trains, pp1-9 (accessed 28/12/2008)

http://en.wikipedia.org/wiki/Island Line Trains, pp1-3 (accessed 28/12/2008)

http://en.wikipedia.org/wiki/Megatrain, pp1-4 (accessed 28/12/2008)

Glossary of terms and abbreviations

ac	Alternating current
ACoRP	Association of Community Rail Partnerships
ATOC	Association of Train Operating Companies
BR	British Railways
BREL	British Rail Engineering Limited
BTP	British Transport Police
CCTV	Closed Circuit Television
CRP	Community Rail Partnership
dc	Direct current
DCS	Down Carriage Sidings
DfT	Department for Transport
DMU	Diesel Multiple-Unit
DVT	Deep Vein Thrombosis
EMU	Electric Multiple-Unit
HC	High Capacity
kWh	Kilowatt-hour
LSWR	London & South Western Railway
MBO	Management Buy Out
OPRAF	Office of Passenger Rail Franchising
ORR	Office of Rail Regulator
ROSCO	Rolling Stock Operating Company
sSRA	Shadow Strategic Rail Authority
SRA	Strategic Rail Authority
SWT	South West Trains
TCD	Traincare Depot
TOC	Train Operating Company
TOPS	Total Operations Processing System
TSO	Trailer Standard Open
UK	United Kingdom
WBV	Whole Body Vibration

Lack of space prevents the inclusion of individual vehicle codes.

Acknowledgements

The author acknowledges the assistance given by the following people, especially my wife Shirley and long-time friend Alun Caddy for their support and never-ending proofreading, without which the publication of this book would not have been possible:

Baker, Stuart
Balmforth, Shirley
Brookes, Peter (*Commercial Timetable Manager SWT*)
Caddy, Alun J.
Clarke, Veronica (*SWT Head of Performance and Train Planning*)
Dickinson, Tony (*Flagship Station Manager, Island Line*)
Field, Peter (*Director London Rail Development, Transport for London*)
Green, Chris
Harper, Jeff (*Depot Manager, Island Line*)
Lee, Jane (*previously head of Media and Public Affairs, South West Trains*)
Lucas, Daniel (*Flagship Station Manager, Waterloo, South West Trains*)
Mackin, Rich (*www.railwayscene.co.uk*)
Marsden, Colin J.
Milligan, Eddie (*Production Services Manager, Siemens Northam TCD*)
Morgan, Jez (*Operational Trainer, SWT Operations and Safety Training Centre*)
Morrison, Brian
Palmer, Stewart (*South West Trains Managing Director, 2006-2009*)
Pomeroy, Andrew ('Pugs') (*Island Line Permanent Way Department*)
Potter, Dave (*SWT Driver Manager, Waterloo*)
Ritchie, Doreen (*South West Trains Duty Manager, Waterloo*)
Rowe, Jim (*Senior Communications Manager, Virgin Trains*)
Siemens UL
Stagecoach Group
Stagecoach South Western Trains Ltd
Stewart, Steven (*Stagecoach Director of Corporate Communications*)
Souter, Brian (*Chief Executive, Stagecoach Group*)
South West Trains Operations and Safety Training Centre
Tucker, Brian (*SWT 'Desiro' Fleet Engineer*)
Virgin Trains
Walker, Steve (*Fleet Director, Siemens Northam TCD*)
Whitehorn, Will (*Virgin Group*)